NO SCHOOL TO-MORROW

FLORA, THE CAT, KNEW THAT LITTLE GIRL WAS ON VACATION

No School To-Morrow

BY

MARGARET ASHMUN

Applewood Books
Carlisle, Massachusetts

This book was originally published in September of 1925.

Foreword © 2014 Amy Wilentz

HC: 978-1-4290-9367-5
PB: 978-1-4290-9365-1

Thank you for purchasing an Applewood book.
Applewood reprints America's lively classics—
books from the past that are still of interest to modern readers.
Our mission is to build a picture of America's past through its primary sources.

To inquire about this edition or to request a free copy
of our current catalog featuring our best-selling books, write to:
Applewood Books
P.O. Box 27
Carlisle, MA 01741
For more complete listings,
visit us on the web at www.awb.com

MANUFACTURED IN THE UNITED STATES OF AMERICA

TO

SALLY AND SAMMY

FOREWORD

CHILDHOOD, MADE PERFECT ON THE PAGE

By Amy Wilentz

Reading is such an improbable idea—a miracle, really. Yet simple squiggles on a page, arranged just so, can convey ideas that change the way we think or introduce to us characters we love for a lifetime. In celebration of reading—and of this weekend's Los Angeles Times Festival of Books—we asked four readers (who also happen to be writers) to celebrate books that mattered in their lives.

My grandfather's house on the New Jersey shore was a huge 1880s double-parlor Victorian with eleven bedrooms, a wraparound porch, and a big green couch in the living room next to the piano. I spent most of my time the summer I turned eight on that couch.

My grandmother would be upstairs in her

air-conditioned room, practicing Mendelssohn on the violin. I could hear it. The men would be at work. My brothers would be out playing or swimming at the beach club, where my mother would sit with her friends around a big white metal table under a beach umbrella, smoking and gossiping.

The reason I loved the couch was that there were two stocked bookcases in the same room, barrister bookcases that my grandfather had bought, along with the books in them, when he got the house in the 1940s. Most of the books were from the 1920s. Here I would sit in my shorts and red PF Flyers and read "My Book House," a series of illustrated children's books. They were good books filled with children's poems and short fairy tales, and I loved them. For a time that summer, I thought these were the best books ever written.

That was, until I found No School To-Morrow, by Margaret Ashmun.

No School To-Morrow was the first "chapter book" I'd ever read. It takes place in a town called Bellville, and its nine-year-old heroine, Louise Martin, was, like me, on summer vacation. Louise goes outside to play. She has a picnic with her friend Anna Fowler. She pats her cat, Flora. She makes her bed and straightens her room. She goes into town with her parents to buy wallpaper. She and Anna build a working stove. They go frogging. They make pan-cakes. Louise watches her mother do the ironing. Louise eats oatmeal and oranges.

Setting it down like that makes the book sound dull, but it was far from dull. Every moment of it shone out for me with the reality of true experi-ence. I lived inside this book and read it over and over. I could escape from Mendelssohn and the beach club into its pages, yet the book was also about my summer, and my friend Nancy across the street, and my parents, and my house. Louise in 1925 (in my childishness, I thought her name was pronounced Loo-whee-sie) was me in 1962. Fol-lowing her, I entered the book in the same way the children in *Mary Poppins* entered the sidewalk paintings. I spent my summer in that book, really in it, rather than in my house on that green couch. Reading has never again been so real for me.

About ten years ago, after a long search, I found a copy of the book on the Internet. In rereading it as an adult, I realized that this plain book, with its modicum of story and its radiant language, was what set me on the path to becoming a writer.

It wasn't just that it helped me understand what a powerful spell a book can cast on the imagina-tion; it was also that its sentences were perfect. Here's one: "So they went back to the lower ground and took off their shoes and stockings on the thick green grass." You can't make a better sentence than that in English, to my mind.

The copy I now own previously belonged to the WPA District No. 4 Pack Horse Library, a New Deal project that sent brigades of young women carrying library books out on foot or by mule to the mountain villages of eastern Kentucky. The names of some of the borrowers of *No School To-Morrow* are on a card that's still in the little manila slip on the back inside cover: Edna Back, Irene Cornett, Bittie Frank Caton, Mildred Bellamy, Mary Nunn, Billy Jane Little, Ruth Glover, Thelma Noble, Betty Gabbard. Hail to you, girls! I like to think of Edna and Mary and Thelma and Bittie and the rest, somewhere in a miners' camp in the dark 1930s, reading about Loo-whee-sie in the sunshine and on the grass, Loo-whee-sie and her stove, her pancakes, her frogs.

Amy Wilentz's most recent book, Farewell, Fred Voodoo: A Letter From Haiti, *won the 2013 National Book Critics Circle Award for autobiography.*

LIST OF ILLUSTRATIONS

Flora, the cat, knew that little girl was on vacation
Frontispiece

FACING
PAGE

When the long vacation lies before you . . . 68

"I'm like a little rabbit scrooching down in here" 182

"Let the scarecrow be teacher," called Eddie . 214

CONTENTS

CHAPTER | PAGE

I. No School 1

II. Pancakes 20

III. Frogs and Fishes 41

IV. Play and Painting 64

V. The Mill Party 92

VI. What Mother Wanted 117

VII. Strawberries 146

VIII. A Treasure from the Attic 175

NO SCHOOL TO-MORROW

CHAPTER I

NO SCHOOL

"Well, Little Girl," said Tall Father, pausing at the kitchen door, where the sunlight was pouring in, "it seems to me I've heard something about your vacation's beginning this morning. What are you going to do all summer, if I may be so bold as to inquire?"

"Play," answered Little Girl, taking another spoonful of oatmeal with a great deal of cream on it. She was sitting up at the leaf of the kitchen table, eating her breakfast, because she was late, and everything had been cleared away before she came down. She hadn't put on her shoes and stockings, and her bare toes were curled round the rungs of her chair.

"Play!" cried Tall Father, as if he had never

heard of such a thing. "Dear me, Mother, is it possible that we have a frivolous young person in our midst?"

"It looks like it," smiled Mother. She went over to the table, and buttoned the last button of Little Girl's blue frock, and then she gave Little Girl a pat on the head as if she couldn't help doing it.

"I'm surprised—and most distressed," said Father, leaning against the doorpost. "What are vacations for, if not to work in?"

Little Girl looked up from her oatmeal. She had to look at Father to tell whether he were joking or not, and even then she couldn't always tell. "Why, Fath-er," she said, "of course vacations are to play in—of course they are!"

"Oh, are they?" asked Father, as if he were more astonished than ever. "Well, how should I know? I never have any."

Little Girl was puzzled. Now that he had mentioned it, she didn't remember that Father ever had a real vacation, when he had nothing to do but play. "Anyway, I'm going to," she said hastily. She helped herself to an orange, and slid down from her chair. She was biting into the orange with white little teeth.

"I continue to be surprised," said Father.

"Don't let him tease you," said Mother. "Are you sure you have had enough breakfast?"

"Yes, Mother," said Little Girl. Mothers always seem to be watching, to see whether one eats enough.

"And what is Flora going to do?" asked Father. Flora was the black-and-white cat. She sat washing her paws in the square of sunshine on the floor.

"Just what she always does," mumbled Little Girl, sucking her orange.

"Perhaps she'll tell us," suggested Father; and when he began to sing:

"Oh, lovely Flora,
    Listen to my lay.
What are your intentions
    This bright and balmy day?
When you are a-roaming
    The barn, or else the house,
Will you, won't you catch us
    A beautiful blue mouse?
Say yes, oh-h-h-h, lovely Flora!"

"Miaouw!" said Flora, not liking the loud tones of Father's voice.

"There! She says *yes,*" said Father, greatly pleased. "A very wise cat. You may look for your blue mouse about lunch time, Louella-Puella." Father called Little Girl by that name because her real name was Louise Ellsworth Martin. *Louise Ellsworth,* put together, made *Louella;* and *Puella,* as some people, if not all, know well, is the Latin for *Little Girl.* Louise was used to being called by a good many different names. Father said that using one name all the time was tiresome.

Louella laid her orange on the table, and took Flora up in her arms. Flora rubbed her head along Louella's shoulder and purred. "Loveliest kitty in the world," whispered Little Girl.

"To the work, to the work," yawned Father, stretching his arms above his head. Sometimes Father was a good deal like a little boy. He walked across the kitchen and through the sitting room and into the little room at the side, which was his study. He was in the habit of writing there all the forenoon, with

the door open. Louise hardly ever dared go
in when he was working, but she liked to look
in and watch him beating away at the keys of
the typewriter, or sitting with his hands
clasped behind his head, staring out of the
window. Once in a while he would groan and
mutter to himself, and run his fingers through
his hair, as if he were trying to do something
that was too hard for him.

This morning Louise wanted to be out of
doors; and so she did not stay to watch Father.
She put Flora carefully down on her four little
white feet. "Do I have to put on my shoes?"
she asked.

"Not unless you want to," said Mother, busy
at the sink. "It's as warm as can be to-day."
It was a June morning and the sun was bright,
but not too hot. It was Monday morning, too,
and school had closed on Friday. You don't
begin to count the days of a vacation until
Sunday is over, because you wouldn't have to
go to school on Sunday anyway. "Have a
good time, Louise," added Mother.

"Yes, I will," answered Louise politely. It
was pleasant in the kitchen, with the bright

rag rugs on the floor, and the bright dishes
in the glass cupboard, and yellow gingham curtains at the windows; but there were dozens of
things to do outside. Out of doors is a wonderful place when you are nine years old and
school is out, and the long vacation lies before
you, going on and on, almost forever. Louise
took her orange again, and went out at the
side door of the kitchen, where Father had
come in. There were little pink roses opening
on the vine that went along the side of the
house. She felt the boards of the steps warm
and smooth against her feet. The wind blew
her hair around her shoulders. "Oh!" she
said to herself, "oh!" She jumped up and
down, just for the happiness of it all. "What
shall I do first?" she thought.

Then, because there were so many things
to choose, and no hurry about any of them,
she decided to let the bucket down into the
well. That was something that Father never
liked to have her do, unless she were very
careful. The bucket hung on a windlass, which
is a sort of log with a handle on it, like the

wringer of a big washing machine. If you let the handle slip, it would go round and round, terribly fast, and then it was best to keep away from it. Louise put the orange down on the grass, and slowly and carefully turned the handle of the windlass backward. The empty bucket went down smoothly. Standing on her tiptoes she could see it swinging and swaying as it sank deeper into the well, where a faint glimmer of sky showed, a long way below. Then with a *chug,* the bucket struck the water. *Chug, chug—gurgle, gurgle—*the bucket was filling through the hole in the bottom that had a hinged valve over it. All at once it sank heavily into the deep water, and lay still. Louella did not intend that it should fill quite to the top. "If I could get just a little in it, I could pull it up," she thought. But it was too late; the bucket was full. She tugged and pulled, thinking that perhaps she was stronger than she had been the last time she tried; but it was of no use. She could not lift the bucket. And then she remembered that Tall Father had told her never to try. "It's

too much for a little Cricket like you," he had
said, frowning. And then he had sung:

"Little Cricket tried to lift
A bucket full of water.
It weighed a ton,
Which was no fun,
And worried Daddy's Daughter."

Louise sighed and let go of the handle of
the windlass. She thought she had better go
on toward the barn. Flora was mewing and
rubbing her soft fur against the little girl's
bare legs.

So Little Girl took up her orange, which
she had laid on the clean, green grass, and she
went on, picking her way down the path, because her feet were soft and tender, and she
felt even the smallest pebble and the tiniest
twig. She hummed a little tune as she walked
along. The raspberry bushes were full of fresh
leaves, almost covering the red stems. The
strawberry bed on the other side of the path
was one big flat space of leaves. There was
no use in looking for strawberries, Louella
knew, for she had hunted all through the patch

only yesterday, and had found only little hard green ones. It seemed as if they were never going to get ripe.

Then Louise was in the barn. Now, this barn was probably the nicest place for little girls to play in that any one has ever seen. You went into it at the side through huge double doors that were wide enough for a load of hay to be driven through. The sunshine streamed in across the plank floor, which was littered with dried grass and straw, and was soft to your bare feet. Above, there was a high roof, where rays of light came through tiny cracks between the shingles, and made long, dusty lines in the shadows. On each side were dusky places which had been stalls for horses and cows in times past; but there were none there now. Louise thought it would have been fun to hear them munch their hay while she played. There was only the little automobile, Ann Eliza, which Father had bought last year from a man who was getting a nicer one. Ann Eliza never munched oats or switched her tail or stamped in her stall, but she was a good little creature for all that.

There was nothing like her for a ride through
the country. She was, on the whole, much
better than a cud-chewing cow, or a tail-switch-
ing horse.

Flora-Puss crouched herself down beside
some barrels and boxes, and began watching
a dark place behind them, with round, steady
eyes which never moved to the right or the
left. "She's after a blue mouse," whispered
Louise; "but I hope she won't catch any, even
a gray one. Poor little things!" As a matter
of fact, Flora hardly ever did catch anything,
for she was too well fed, and did not feel
much interested in hunting. Before Louise
had finished her orange, Flora had tucked her
toes under her and settled down for a doze.

Louise threw her orange skin out at the far
side of the barn, where it fell among burdocks
and thistles. Doves were cooing and murmur-
ing up in the gable. Once Father had taken
Little Girl away up to the doves' nests (he
had made a kind of ladder of small boards
nailed to the side of the barn, inside), and
had shown her the queer, naked, skinny squabs,
with their bright, scared eyes peering over the

side of the nest. Little Girl had been disappointed, because she had supposed that everything that was a baby was pretty, and she was sure that baby doves would be the prettiest of all. "Oo-oo, Father," she had called, "do you think the mother dove imagines *those* are pretty? Do you think she *can?*"

"I shouldn't wonder," Father had said. "As far as I can make out, every mother thinks her squabs are the loveliest things in the world, no matter if they're as red and bald and wrinkled as you were when you were a baby dove, my dear Louella."

Louella had not known exactly what he meant, and she thought about it now, as she sat on an overturned water pail. "I suppose they've got some clothes on by this time— feathers, I mean," she said. "But it doesn't matter much, because it's so warm." She would have liked to climb up and look at them, but Father had told her that she must never do it unless he were with her. Fathers were so careful of their children!

Louise began to play a game with herself, which she liked to play when she was alone.

It was "Making Calls." She pulled boxes and pails and an oil can about on the barn floor, to serve for seats and people sitting around a parlor. She found all at once that she had on a long pink silk dress covered with spangles, that swished and rustled when she walked, and white satin slippers. An old straw hat of Father's was hanging on a peg, and when she put it on, it became a beautiful velvet hat with long pink plumes that hung down to her shoulders. And when she took up a stick and put a piece of paper at the end, it turned out to be a parasol with lace around the edge. Any little girl who loves to "make believe" will understand just how these things happened.

Louise, finding herself so richly dressed, was ready to make a call on Mrs. Montgomery. This was a name that Father had taught her. Louise's name was now Mrs. Periwinkle.

Louise rang the bell at Mrs. Montgomery's door—that is, she tapped on the oil can with the handle of her parasol. Mrs. Montgomery was slow in coming to the door, and Mrs. Periwinkle had to ring again.

At last Mrs. Montgomery came to the door quite out of breath. She shook hands with Louella—that is, with Mrs. Periwinkle—holding her hand very high and using just the tips of her fingers. "Oh, I'm so sorry I was slow," said the hostess. "I was just putting the baby to bed for his nap."

"Indeed," said Mrs. Periwinkle, putting down her parasol (she had to pull the piece of paper off and hide it behind a barrel). "You *were* rather slow." She switched her long pink silk skirt as she walked into the hall. "I suppose the baby was yelling—I mean crying."

"No, not at all," said Mrs. Montgomery. "He never cries. He's such a good child. All my children are good. Won't you sit down, Mrs. Periwinkle?"

Louella sat down on a cracker box and spread her pink silk skirt around her, and stuck out her white satin slippers. She saw that Mrs. Montgomery had on a bright blue velvet dress trimmed with little red satin roses. It was not so grand as Mrs. Periwinkle's and of course there was no hat to go with it. "How is your husband, Mrs. Mont-gom-ery?" asked the caller.

"Oh, he's very well," answered the other lady in a high voice. "He's gone to town to-day in our car-r, and he's going to buy me another yellow silk ball dress and a thermos bottle, so we can go on picnics. Don't you just love picnics, Mrs. Periwinkle?"

"I like 'em when I can go in wading," said Mrs. Periwinkle in a voice which sounded too much like Louella's. "I mean, I like picnics ever so much, Mrs. Mont-gom-ery."

"Won't you have some tea?" said the hostess quickly. She poured out some tea from an empty varnish bottle which stood on a shelf.

"I'd just love to have some," said the caller, leaning her parasol against a barrel. She took the tea, put in cream and sugar, and then drank very elegantly, holding her little finger out from her hand. "This is delicious tea, Mrs. Mont-gom-ery," she said. "Where do you buy your tea?"

good tea. Won't you have a frosted cake, Mrs. Periwinkle?"

"Why-y, perhaps I will. Thank you. I'll take this one with the nuts on it."

Mrs. Periwinkle was just about to eat the tempting cake with icing and nuts, which her hostess had passed to her on a shingle, when a voice sounded from the barn door. "Why, Louie Martin, who are you talking to? I don't see a soul!" There stood Anna Fowler, as neat as could be in her starched gingham dress and long black stockings and black shoes. She even had on a hat.

Louise felt rather foolish. "I was just playing," she said. Anna never seemed to care much for the "make-believe" kind of plays. She always wanted to do what she called "real" things. Louise was sorry that Anna had come just at the minute that the make-believe frosted cake was to be eaten, though she was fond of Anna and usually glad to see her.

"What have you got on?" asked the caller, looking at the old straw hat, which a moment before had been a velvet hat with long pink plumes.

"I—I put on Father's old hat. I was just pretending," stammered Louise. It was hard to explain such things to Anna. Louise took the hat off and hung it up on the peg. "What do you want to play?" she said in a hurry, because she didn't want Anna to ask anything more about what she had been doing. Louise had heard her mother say that Anna was "active and practical."

"I'd like to go for wintergreens," said Anna.

"How long can you stay?" asked Louise.

"Only a few minutes, while my father goes to the store," answered Anna. "Of course we can't go for wintergreens. There isn't time."

"No," said Louise, "but we can do something else."

"We might make the stove in our play-house," said Anna. The girls were laying out a playhouse under the farthest apple trees in the orchard on the hill.

"But I haven't any shoes on," objected Louise, "and by the time I get 'em on you'll almost have to go."

"Oh, dear," sighed Anna. "Well, let's swing, then. Do you want to go first?"

"Oh, no." Louise was always polite to her visitors, and anyhow she did not care to swing in the same way that Anna did. The long, heavy ropes of the swing hung near at hand, with a strong board seat notched at the sides, so that it could not slip. Anna climbed into the swing and stood up, her solid little shoes placed firmly on the board seat.

"Whoo-oo!" she cried. "Here we go!" She made her knees go up and down as if she were pumping, while she held hard to the ropes. Far back and forth she swung, faster and faster, until Louise looked on, half frightened.

"How can you swing so high?" she called, as if Anna were a long way off.

"Pooh! Who's afraid?" called Anna. There was hardly anything that she was afraid of, and she never seemed to get hurt, either. "I just love it. It's like flying." Her brown hair was blowing in the warm wind which came through the barn doors, and her dark eyes were shining with enjoyment. After a

while, she let the swing move more slowly.
"Don't you want to get in now?" she said.
"Oh, no," said Louise again. She liked to
have Anna swing if she wanted to; so Anna
swung and swung, and Louise sat on the water
pail and watched her. Once or twice she
thought of the little play cake which she had
been about to eat when Anna came. And then
there was Mother coming down the long path
from the house with a tray. "Oo-oo! Something to eat!" cried Louise, as if she had had
to go without her breakfast. "Mm-m, Anna,
Mother's bringing something."

Anna stopped swinging and jumped down.
Both girls ran to the barn door. "I thought
you might want a bite," said Mother, smiling.
She looked a good deal like a girl in her short
pink house dress and white apron. She held
the tray down, so that the girls could see.
There was a white pitcher with blue stripes
around it, full of creamy milk; and there were
two little glasses and a bright orange plate
with ginger cookies on it. Mother put the tray
down on a barrel, and poured two glasses of
milk and passed them to the girls.

"Aren't you going to have some, Mother?" asked Louise.

"No, not now," said Mother. "Your father said he'd come right back, didn't he, Anna? It's too bad that you can't stay longer."

"Mother wants me to take care of Bobby," answered Anna, biting into a cookie. "But I can come again."

"Come to-morrow," said Louise eagerly. "There's no school to-morrow!"

"We can just play and play," said Anna, "because there isn't any school. We can make a stove in our playhouse, and build a fire, and cook real things to eat."

A *honk-honk* came from the gate. "Mr. Fowler is here. Too bad," said Mother. "We're sorry you couldn't stay a little longer."

Anna gulped the last of her milk. "I'm coming, Father," she called shrilly. She ran up the path as fast as she could go, but in the middle she turned and waved her hand. "I'll be over to-morrow. No school! No school!"

CHAPTER II

PANCAKES

The next morning, when Little Girl woke up in her own room with the queer wriggly wall paper, she saw that the sky was not so bright as it had been the day before. She washed and dressed herself quickly, and ran downstairs with her shoes in her hand. In the kitchen, Mother was putting some toast and warm milk and a poached egg on a tray that had a yellow linen cloth over it. "Oh, there you are, Louella," she said. "I was going to take the tray up to you."

"You needn't ever do that," said Louella-Puella, rather ashamed of being late again, though Mother was always pleased to have her get a great deal of sleep.

"I'll put it on the little stand in the sitting room," said Mother.

Father was at his work in his study, but

he called out, "Top o' the morning, Lady Bird."

"Top o' the morning, Poppy," called Lady Bird, though she never had found out what the words meant.

She loved to have her breakfast tray on the little low stand in the sitting room. The old-fashioned clock with the painted glass front ticked slowly and quietly, as if there were no hurry about anything; Father's typewriter clicked and rattled; and Flora lay on the couch, purring as loudly as any cat could purr. But in spite of all those little sounds, everything seemed peaceful and content. As Louella ate her breakfast, she made believe that she was in the big hotel that Father had told her about, that he had stayed in when he was in New York.

She carried the tray to the kitchen when she had finished, and Mother said, "Now for the chicks." She was mixing scraps of bread and some corn meal with water and sour milk. Louella slipped on her shoes and went out with Mother. The sky was cloudy and the air was damp. The newest little chicks were running around their tent-shaped coop, and the old hen was sticking her red head out between the slats and clucking anxiously.

Mother let Louella scatter the food on a clean board and on the grass. The little round balls of fluff went running and cheeping, picking up tiny bits of food with their yellow bills. "Do you want to take one up, Louise?" said Mother. "Be very careful."

Louise reached out quickly and took one up in her hands. It struggled and then lay still, its small, clean legs hanging down, its panting little body held close under her fingers. "Why, there's almost nothing to it, Mother," said Louise. "It's such a wee bit of a thing; I don't want to frighten it." She put the chick down, and it ran and hid under its mother's feathers, while the old hen clucked loudly, to show what she thought of little girls who caught baby chickens and held them.

They went on to the other coops, where the chickens were larger, then to the long, fenced-in runway where the big hens and roosters were imprisoned. Father had to keep them there most of the day, so that they would not spoil the garden and eat up the berries. He usually let them out late in the afternoon and watched to keep them out of mischief.

As Louise and her mother went toward the house, they stopped and looked off down the hill at the little village below. "There's a lovely soft mist on everything," said Mother. "I shouldn't wonder if it would rain."

The Martins lived at the top of a low hill above the village of Bellville. You could look down from the front porch and see the river among the trees, and the two bridges, and the red mill, and a flock of white houses along the main street, which followed the course of the river. You couldn't quite see Mr. Rickman's store, nor the blacksmith shop (which was really a place for Ford cars to be mended), but you knew where they were. The church and the schoolhouse were up on the hill, right near where Louise lived. She could look out at the kitchen window and see the schoolhouse windows, when the leaves were not too thick on the trees and bushes that stood between. Beyond the schoolhouse was the church, with a small four-pointed tower.

Little Girl's father was named Gordon
Graham Martin. He had brought Mother and
Little Girl to Bellville more than a year
before. You see, Father wanted to write
books, and when he was working in an office,
he didn't have time to write; and so he had
left the city and come to the country and
bought this old house with three acres of land
around it. Buying the house, though it didn't
cost much, had taken nearly all the money he
had. He wrote things (which he didn't sell
very often), and he raised fruit and vegetables, which he said sold better than his writing, and at least they could eat the things
that grew, if they couldn't eat the things that
he wrote.

You might think that the Martins were
poor, but they weren't. They had the house
and barn and three acres of land; and Father
had Mother and Louella-Puella, and Mother
had Father and Louella, and Louella had
Father and Mother and Flora. So you see
they were really very rich, even if they didn't
have much money.

Louella and her mother went into the house,

and Louella wiped the dishes, and fed Flora, and made her own bed, and straightened everything in her room. The washing had come home, all white and fresh in a basket, and Louella helped her mother sort the things out, and then she looked on while Mrs. Martin sprinkled them and rolled them up, ready for ironing.

"It gets grayer and grayer," said Mrs. Martin.

"Oh, dear!" said Louella. "Anna and I were going to play and play."

Mother got out the ironing board and heated the irons. The day was cool, so that it was not unpleasantly hot in the kitchen. It was almost eleven o'clock when Anna came, and she had hardly arrived before a few drops of rain began to fall. In ten minutes the rain was pelting against the west side of the house, and Mother was running to shut the windows.

"Oh, dear!" said Anna, almost crying. "Louise, we might just as well have to go to school. Now we can't make our stove in the orchard and cook things."

"Oh, dear!" sighed Louise, feeling as gloomy as Anna looked.

"I thought of the grandest way to make it," Anna went on; "with stones and bricks, and that piece of tin that we found, and a real little stovepipe out of that tile left from the sink drain."

"It would have been the most fun," said Louise, though she was not quite so wild about making things as Anna was.

The two girls stood at the window, pouting. Mother was ironing the lunch napkins very carefully. "Can't you think of something else to do?" she asked.

"No, ma'am, not anything as nice as that," answered Anna.

"I can't think of *anything*," said Louella.

Mother thought for a minute, and then she said, "I know a plan."

"Oh, what?" asked both the girls. Mrs. Martin's plans were always interesting.

"Why not cook in the woodshed?"

"How? How?" Both girls crowded against the ironing board. "You mean use the stove in there, Mommy?" asked Louise.

"Yes, that's what I mean." There was an old stove in the woodshed which had been put there to wash with, but it was hardly ever used, because the washing was sent out of the house. In the hot days of summer, Mother used it for ironing or making jam. "I am sure you can cook something on that," said Mrs. Martin.

"Oh, good, goody!" Little Girl danced up and down. Her heels clattered on the floor.

Anna ran and threw open the door into the woodshed. "It's just as good as the stove we were going to make," she cried. "I believe it's better." The two girls ran down the two steps into the big shed, where the rain was pounding on the thin roof with the sound of hammers.

"Tell us, tell us," called Louise, putting her head back into the kitchen.

"Well, you must take the things off the stove, and then build the fire yourselves, and get it going nicely, and then you may cook ____."

"*Real* things?" asked Anna. Her voice almost trembled with eagerness. Anna did dearly love to do real things.

"Yes, real ones," laughed Mrs. Martin, "as solid as can be."

"What?" asked both girls in chorus.

"I'll tell you when the fire is made."

The girls scampered to pull the papers and the clothespin box and other articles off the stove, and to wipe it clean with a cloth.

"Mother, how do you build a fire?" asked Louise breathlessly.

"You've seen it done, dear."

"Yes, but I never noticed."

Mother raised her voice so that she could go on ironing while she told the girls what to do. "See that the damper in the stovepipe is open—that is, straight up and down." There was a scramble while Anna stood on a chair to turn the damper. "Take off the two lids in front." Each girl lifted one. "Is the stove clean?"

"Yes," they answered together.

"Then take some pieces of paper and crumple them up—not too much. Put them in the bottom of the stove, on the grate. Then put in some chips and some dry pieces of kindling." Each girl put in both chips and kindling. "Then some larger pieces of dry wood. Then light it."

Louise wanted to light it, but she had to be polite. "I'll let Anna do it because she's company," she said.

Anna was jumping with happiness. She scratched the match on a brick, and it sputtered and went out, because her fingers were so unsteady. Louise was all impatience. Anna scratched another match. Mother watched from the doorway. "There! hold it under the papers and light them." *Flare* went the papers. A line of blue smoke came from under the lids. "Oh, bother!" cried Mrs. Martin. "I hope it isn't going to smoke. It might, on a wet day like this." More smoke poured out. "Shut the front a little more." They all stood waiting to see what the stove was going to do. The smoke grew thinner, faded, and disappeared. The roar of the fire could be heard above the thumping of the rain. "There! it's all right," said Mother with relief.

"Hooray!" cried Anna.

The fire was now burning steadily, and the heat could be felt round the stove. "We built a fire," said Louise. "I didn't suppose we could."

"I thought we could," said Anna. "Now what are we going to cook?"

"Pancakes," said Mrs. Martin. "Will that suit?"

"Will it? I should say so. I just love pancakes!" cried Anna.

"I do, too," said Louise. "But you'll have to tell us how to make them, Mother."

"You two girls may have my sewing table in the woodshed, and cook your own dinner and eat it there," said Mother. "You can have a real little party of your own, and do just as you like."

"That'll be lots of fun," said Anna. "We'll have to get things ready first."

The table was pulled and hurried to the woodshed. There was a smooth floor around two sides, and the wood had been piled in one corner. A little tablecloth and some dishes were put upon the table. The fire was crackling and burning brightly. There were two win-

dows in the woodshed, and at each one the
rain poured down the glass, so that nothing
could be seen but water and a blur of green
from the trees.

The girls were on tiptoe with excitement.
"Get a cup of sour milk," said Mother. "Louise, you know where it is, in the kitchen cupboard." Louise ran to get the pitcher and
pour out a cup of the thick sour milk. "Anna
may put another stick of wood into the stove.
One egg—Anna may get that from the basket
in the pantry. Then the box of baking soda,
the salt, the flour, and a little corn meal."

"That's what we give the little chickens,"
said Anna.

"Well, you're my little chickens," answered
Mrs. Martin. "Put some water on the stove
to heat—a little in a basin. Get the griddle,
Little Girl."

"It's heavy," said Little Girl, lifting it from
its nail behind the stove. "We want the pancake turner, too, don't we?"

"Yes, and some fat in that yellow bowl, and
the fork with the cloth on the end, for a
greaser."

The girls ran here and there, getting the wrong things, bumping into each other, laughing and scurrying, and quickly bringing together in the shed the things which they would need for their party. The griddle was put on the stove, and the biggest yellow bowl was set out to stir the batter in.

"Oh, sirup!" cried Little Girl.

"To be sure!" exclaimed Mother. "Get some brown sugar out of the cupboard, put nearly a cupful in a basin, and pour just a tiny bit of water on it—not more than two tablespoonfuls." One girl handled the sugar and one the water, and they both carried the basin to the stove.

"I think it would be nice to have some scrambled eggs with the pancakes," said Mrs. Martin. The girls agreed that it would.

The old pine table in the woodshed was covered with needful articles, and the little sewing table was neatly set. Mother was going on with her ironing.

"We forgot something. We must have some flowers on our table," said Louise. "Mother always has 'em." She opened the outside door of the shed and snatched a handful of the white-flowered mayweed growing at the edge of the walk. She got her head wet and splashed the front of her dress, but she did not mind. She put the flowers in a glass in the middle of the table. "Now we're all ready to begin."

"Put the sour milk into the big bowl," called Mother. Anna soberly poured it in. "Break the egg into the milk." Louise's hands slipped as she handled the egg. Oh, the excitement of breaking it and seeing the yellow yolk and glassy white fall into the milk! "Oh, dear, Mother, I've got pieces of shell in it! I'm sure you never do that."

"Never mind. Fish them out with a spoon," called Mrs. Martin cheerfully. "Stir up the egg."

"You stir, Anna. Oh, it's all streaky."

"A pinch of salt. And then three-quarters of a teaspoonful of soda in a cup. Pour on a little hot water, stir it up, and pour it into the milk and egg."

The girls did as they were told. "Whew! It fizzes!" shouted Louise.

"I can hear it!" shrieked Anna. "It's just as loud."

"It should fizz. Now the flour. Sift a little in." They had to take turns at the sifting, because it was too much fun for either of them to miss. "A half a cup of corn meal—stir it in slowly." Mother came to inspect the batter. "Rather thin. Just a little more flour. Now stir it so that it will be smooth. Goodness, how the rain pours down!"

"We don't care. It's lovely in here," said Anna, beaming. "How I love to cook, and Mother will hardly ever let me. I always have to take care of Bobby while she cooks."

"You fry the first one," said Louise generously. The griddle was smoking a little. It was a breathless moment when the first big spoonful of the batter dropped, sizzling, on the griddle. It was an equally anxious one when the round, bubbling cake was turned. It spattered a bit when it went over, but it kept its shape and showed a tempting brown on the cooked side.

While it was cooking, the girls gave their attention to scrambling the eggs.

They broke the yolks, but "It doesn't make any difference," said Anna, "as long as we're going to scramble them, anyhow."

Now more cakes went on the griddle, and the first one was put on the warm plate, to keep the others from cooling. "I just have to turn some," said Louise. "Isn't it fun to hear them go *flop?*"

"That's why they're called flapjacks," called Mother. She was putting away her ironing, to get dinner for Father.

At last there was the happiness of sitting down at the little table in the woodshed. The cooks were flushed and tired with their exertions, but they were proud and delighted with what they had done. The pancakes were almost (perhaps quite) as good as Mother's. "Oh, you must have a taste, Mommy, with the sirup," said Louise. "It's dee-licious!" And Mother said that it was.

Father came out into the kitchen, humming and sniffing. "I say!" He stood in the woodshed doorway, staring down. "Can I believe my eyes?" Then he began to sing, to the tune of "School Days":

"Pancakes, pancakes,
  Dear old-fashioned pancakes!
Sometimes they're soggy and heavy as lead,
Sometimes they're crispy and light, instead.
Pancakes, pancakes——"

"Oh, Father, don't sing," begged Louise.

"Well, I like that!" said Father. "Asking me not to sing! Don't you like singing, Louella Pancake?"

"Yes, I like singing," said Louella, "but I don't like that noise. I want to tell you," she went on proudly, "that we did everything ourselves, every bit of it."

"Did you, really?" said Father; and now he didn't laugh, but he looked sober and proud. "I think that was pretty good for two little ladies, don't you, Mother?"

"Yes, I do," said Mother, and she looked as pleased as Father. Then Louella must jump up and cook a cake for Father and give it to him all brown and hot, with sirup on it. "Is it soggy and heavy as lead?" she asked, when he was eating it.

"It's the best I ever ate," said Father.

"Well, you two do manage to have the best times."

"Mother thought of it," said Louella.

"Cooking is the most fun there is," put in Anna.

"Aren't you glad it rained?" said Father.

"Yes, yes, yes," answered the girls.

Even heating a kettle of water on the stove and washing the dishes was fun, and putting the things away. But afterward they were glad to sit down and dress dolls quietly for an hour or two. Mother worked in the kitchen and Father went back to his writing. The rain grew less and less, and finally the sun came out. By that time Anna had to go home (her father called for her again). Louella went to the door of her father's writing room called "the study" and knocked, saying with great politeness, "May I come in, Daddy?" If Tall Father were in his study after three o'clock, Louise dared to go in. Father said something in French that meant, "Come in, Little Lamb." So Louella went in, and Father showed her how to write on the typewriter. She tried to write "I love Tall Father," and when she had finished, it looked like this:

I l*cve tA!l xF%thor$

Louella and Father both laughed so much that Mother came in to see what was going on. She laughed, too, when she saw what Louise had written.

"How does it go?" asked Mother, meaning the book which Father was writing.

"Pretty well, to-day," was the answer. "I begin to see the end."

Father was sitting in the chair at the typewriter, and Mother put her hand on his head, just as she did sometimes on Louella's.

"Now *I'm* going to play in the woodshed," said Father. Louella knew that he wanted to finish cutting some long, strong sticks for use in the garden. So she went to the woodshed with him to see him work. The fire had gone out and the door was open, and it was cool and dry in the shed. Father cut some of the sticks from a long pine board, and smoothed them off with a knife, and sharpened one end to stick into the ground. They were to hold up the bean and tomato vines, so that they should not get beaten down along the ground when it rained. When he had finished, he took a new shingle, and cut it out with his knife into the shape he wanted. Then he took some red paint from a can on the shelf, and then some brown paint, and a dash or two of black, and there was a saucy bird. "It's to go on the end of a stick," said Father, as he put it up to dry. "And won't it look nice in our green garden? I hope it will scare the greedy robins away." Louella, with Flora in her lap, sat and watched him until he was ready to go and let the chickens out, and work in the garden while he kept them where they belonged, in the grass and around the barn.

After supper Louella was so tired that she had to go to bed early. Mother lighted a candle in the brass candlestick, and Louella kissed Father, who said, "Good night, my darling," and Mother and Louella went upstairs. It was warm and still, and the rain was falling softly, pattering on the leaves of the cherry tree beside the house. The tree toads were singing with their small, shrill noise. They made Louise think of a poem which Father had written for her, and she said it aloud while Mother turned down the bed:

"A little toad
Sat in the road,
   To rest from many hops.
But to his pain
The cold, wet rain
   Came down in dribbling drops.

At last he spied
A toadstool wide,
   And quickly hopped in under.
'Hurrah!' said he,
'From rain I'm free,
   And also safe from thunder!' "

When Little Girl was undressed and had said her prayers, and was cuddled in bed, Mother sat by the window in the low willow chair. It grew bluer and bluer outside, and a robin burst into a loud calling song. And then Little Girl was fast asleep.

CHAPTER III

When Anna came the next day, it was so warm and bright that the two little girls did something which they hadn't expected to do. "Oh, Mommy, mayn't we go and play behind the old foundry, and wade?" said Louise.

And Mother said, "Yes; but of course you'll be careful and not go where the deep water is."

"We'll just go behind the old foundry," said Anna, who was rather unwilling to give up her plan for making a play stove, but liked wading, too, and was glad to go with Louise.

The foundry was a big, empty red building which had been used years ago for some sort of work that the girls did not understand; beside it was the flume (the long board box which brought the water to the mill, where it fell down in a great white waterfall). Behind the foundry were little shallow streams which were made by the spurts of water that trickled out of the cracks in the flume. These little streams were perfectly safe for children to wade in, because they were not wide nor deep.

"May we put up a lunch?" asked Louise. "Anna has brought some roll jelly cake in a box. Show Mother, Anna."

"My mother said we could always have a picnic lunch, whatever else we did," explained Anna, showing the fat roll of cake with little red circles of jam showing at the ends.

"Can you make the sandwiches yourselves?" asked Mrs. Martin.

"Yes, yes," said the girls. "What kind?"

"Peanut butter, and two or three with crisp, fried bacon."

"You do think of the nicest things," cried Louise. There was great excitement while the bacon was being fried and put between slices of bread. The sandwiches and two oranges and two bananas and the box of jelly cake were all packed in a basket with a handle. The girls took with them also two small shovels which Father had bought last year, and a tiny tin pail "to catch things in."

"Be good girls," said Mother. They were
not going far—in fact, she could almost see
them from the front porch, if the big red
foundry had not been in the way.

They trotted off happily with their load.
They went down the hill, along the pebbled
path, for there were no wooden sidewalks in
Bellville; and then they crossed the big bridge
and turned into the path along the race. There
was a narrow footbridge which they could have
crossed, but their mothers did not like to have
them use it. Now they had come to the old
deserted building. It stood up on posts, instead of having a stone foundation, so that
you could see under one long side of it. Sometimes you could see something moving under
there, but it was always a hen or a cat or one
of Mr. Alford's sheep.

Once behind the building, the girls felt
happy and safe. On one side there was the
big, quiet foundry and the high wooden flume
with its mossy, water-soaked sides, and the
rills trickling down; and farther on there was
the mill, from which a steady rumbling
sounded. On the other side was a green

meadow where two Jersey cows were feeding.
Beyond that were the river with willows droop-
ing over it, and a few white houses and big
barns.

"How nice and *alone* it is here," said Louise. "We can do anything we like. Hear the
birds sing! Oh, we must look at our sparrow's
nest." In a bush close up against the bank,
where it sloped down from the foundry, there
was a song sparrow's nest. Slowly and carefully the girls climbed up the grassy bank.
The mother bird fluttered from the nest as
they approached. "Don't be scared. We
won't hurt you," called Louise in her softest
tone.

"Oh, maybe there are little birds," said
Anna.

Sure enough, there were three little grayish
creatures with big, wide-open mouths and
skinny, yellow necks. The girls couldn't help
laughing to see the gaping beaks waiting to
be filled. "I wish we dared put something
in," said Anna; "some bread or something.
But it might not be the right sort of stuff."

"No," said Louise. "Father says the mother bird knows best what to feed her children."

The mother bird was hopping and twittering on a branch just above her babies. "We wouldn't hurt 'em for anything," said Anna; "little bits of things like that."

"I guess she knows we wouldn't," said Louise. She wanted to put out her hand and touch the queer little birds. She started to put it slowly toward the nest, but the mother bird fluttered her wings and looked so frightened that the little girl stopped. "Come on," she said; "there's no use in bothering her."

So they went back to the lower ground and took off their shoes and stockings on the thick green grass. There were flowers in the grass —short-stemmed purple violets, and tiny white violets with purple veins, and wild strawberry blossoms. Anna was first to put her feet into the water. "Oh!" she squealed, "it's warm and lovely." They waded back and forth, digging their toes into the soft white sand at the bottom of the stream. Then they jumped from one little green island to another, laughing when their feet slipped and went into the bright, clear water.

"Now let's make an aquarium," suggested Louise.

"Let's," said Anna.

They found a pool about twice as big as a dishpan, at the edge of the brook, and they both took shovels and made it deeper. They waited for the water to get clear again, and then they laid white pebbles and shells all over the bottom, and banked it around with turf and flowers, so that they had a pretty little pond. "Now for the fish and things," said Louise.

They watched until they saw a tiny crab scuttling backward along the bottom of the stream. Swoop! Anna had him in the tin pail. They held him up to look at him. He had a gray-green back with overlapping scales on it, and long, pinching claws which waved wildly before him. His eyes were reddish, and they seemed to bulge out of his head. "He's funny, isn't he?" said Anna. "I wonder if he's scared. I don't think he knows

enough to be. Anyhow, nothing's going to
happen to him.''

They overturned the pail into the pool, and
let him go sliding among the white stones and
shells. He crawled around cheerfully enough.
''Now for some minnies,'' said Anna.

There were hundreds of minnows darting
here and there in the deeper places of the
stream. It seemed easy to get them, but when
one of the girls would dip the pail down
swiftly, the fish would be gone in a second,
and only water and sand would come up in the
pail. ''I caught one, I caught one!'' cried
Louise at last. There were two pretty fish
swimming this way and that in the pail, each
about two inches long.

''They're nice,'' said Anna, peering at them,
''but it's too bad they aren't goldfish.''

''I like 'em as they are,'' said Louise. She
let them slip into the aquarium, where they
flirted their tails at the crab and swirled about,
as happy as you please.

After trying a long time, Anna caught three
more, and Louise caught one; so there were
fish enough in the aquarium. ''Another crab

would be a good thing," sighed Anna. "Let's
look all the way up and down, and see what
we can find." All at once she gave a whoop,
and called, "Oh, Louie, Louie!"

Louise came running. "What is it?"

"Look, look!" Anna held out her hand. On
it was sprawling a tiny turtle not as big as a
fifty-cent piece. He was a beautiful fellow,
with dark brown shell, marked with bright red.
Underneath he was yellow, and his four little
legs were marked with paler yellow. "He has
the teeniest little claws you ever saw," said
Anna. "Ugh, they tickle." The turtle was
trying to crawl out of her hand. "He has
the funniest little black eyes and the crossest-
looking mouth!"

They could hardly put him down to let him
swim in the aquarium. But they built a mound
of stones in the middle of the pool for him
to sit on, and he climbed up and sat sunning
himself as if he liked his new home. When
Anna stroked his back with her finger, he
sidled down into the water and swam around
the pool with his legs spread wide. "He'll get
away if we don't watch him," said Anna, who

valued her prize beyond words. But he climbed up on the stones again and the girls went to hunt for more treasures. They found another crab, and several clams and snails, hidden away in their shells, and two big, round polliwogs, with tails.

"We ought to have a frog," said Louise. "We have crabs and fish and snails and clams and polliwogs and a turtle, but a frog would be just the thing. There are lots of them around, but they're so hard to catch."

"I guess I can get one," said Anna. She ran up and down until she saw a spotted frog jumping away from her in the grass. It took a good deal of leaping and grabbing and squealing before she finally had him in her hand. His little green and white feet stuck out between her fingers, but she held him fast, without hurting him, and placed him gently in the pool. "I hope he won't hop right out," she whispered, as if the frog could understand. He didn't. After swimming about, he climbed up on the turtle's tower and sat in the sun.

The girls stood and looked with pride at their aquarium. "It's too lovely for anything,'' said Louise, bending down to see the fishes and the snails, and the wee white violets in the grass at the edge of the pool. Just then Mr. Frog gave a great jump, and went *plump* into the stream, where he swam off, jerking his long legs as if they were on wires.

"I think he might stay,'' said Anna, pouting; "but I'm not going to run after him. I'm hungry.''

"Goodness! I'm hungry, too,'' said Louise. "It must be past noon. We can't tell what time it is when the school bell doesn't ring.''

"There goes Mr. Alford across the bridge,'' sad Anna. "He always goes home just after twelve.''

They took their basket and spread out the tea towel that covered it. Out came the sandwiches and the fruit and the bottle of milk with the two paper cups. How good the peanut butter sandwiches were, and the crisp and crunching bacon between the slices of bread! The jelly cake, which Anna's mother had made that morning, was delicate and delicious. Oranges and bananas made the best sort of dessert for an outdoor meal. When they had finished, they washed their hands and made leaf wreaths and blew loud, squawking blasts on blades of grass. Louise went to gather some tall irises for her mother.

A step sounded on the stones behind the foundry, and the girls looked at each other, startled. They saw Mr. Martin coming from behind the building. "Hello, chicks," he called. "I thought I'd just see how you were getting along."

"We're all right, Father," said Louise, running to meet him, "and you must see our aquarium."

"Splendid!" cried Father, when he had seen the little pool and its living inhabitants. He leaned over to look more closely. "Fish, crabs, snails, clams, and a real live turtle. I declare, I think that's fine." Then he began to sing:

"Oh, the fish walk around
  With their feet on the ground;
  With their feet on the ground,
  The fish walk around.
  Feet on the ground,
  Feet on the ground,
  The fish walk around
  With their feet on the ground——"

"Oh, Father, listen," said Louise impatiently. She had heard that song before.

"Oh, Mr. Martin, we had a frog, but he got away," explained Anna in a loud voice. "He wouldn't stay in the aquarium."

"I don't know that I blame him," said Mr. Martin, "when he had all this big meadow and the little streams and the river to play in. But we'll have a frog, just to finish up with. Hi, there, Mr. Frog, you're wanted." He had seen a green-spotted frog under a clump of grass. The frog hopped, and Father jumped, and away they went across the end of the meadow, Father's long legs sprawling here and there in the grass and reeds. Louise and Anna laughed to see the chase.

Then Mr. Martin came back with the froggie held carefully in his grasp. "Now, sir," said he, "will you go politely into these young ladies' aquarium, or will you not?"

"I will, yes, indeed I will," said the frog in a tiny voice. (Anna and Louise hardly knew whether the frog was speaking, or whether Father was saying the words out of the side of his mouth.)

"All right, sir," said Father. "That's a nice gentlemanly frog."

"I always try to be a gentleman," said the frog.

"Very well, sir. In you go." Father put the frog into the pool, where the little fellow swam around the edge, kicking his legs out in his queer, jerky way. "It's a beautiful aquarium," said Father, and you could see that he was as delighted with it as the girls were, for Father was such a boy, himself.

"Frogs and fishes, and fishes and frogs,
And clams and snails and pollyannawogs,"

sang Father.

Out jumped Mr. Frog with a flying leap which landed him a long way from the edge of the pool. "Oo-oo! he's gone!" cried Louise.

"That's just his way of saying that it's time for us to go home," remarked Father. "Let's go. But first we must let all these little fellows go free."

"Yes, we always do," said Louella. "Now, see, we dig a channel out into the stream, so that they can get away."

The girls took their shovels and dug an opening from the aquarium to the little brook. The fish darted through it, but the crabs took their time. It hardly mattered to them where they were.

"I want to take the turtle home," said Anna, picking up the small brown creature and holding him on her palm.

Louise looked at her father with a troubled face. "Oh, I don't believe I would, Anna," said Mr. Martin. "What could you do with him?"

"Put him in a dish of water," answered Anna.

"I don't believe he would be half as happy as he would crawling around here in the grass and mud," said Mr. Martin. "Do you— really?"

Anna shook her head. "N-no, maybe not," she replied. "I guess I'll leave him." She put the turtle down at the edge of the stream, and he sat there without moving, while Father helped the girls to pack their basket. He finished the last piece of the roll jelly cake "so that they wouldn't have to carry it home," as he said.

Louise ran to get the irises which she had picked for her mother. She had put the ends of the stems into water to keep the flowers fresh. Father carried the basket and the shovels, Louise carried the irises, and Anna carried the pail.

They had to stop and peep at the sparrow's nest again, but the mother bird was sitting over her babies, and they did not want to disturb her. So they trudged home in the warm sun, up the hill, and past the church and the schoolhouse. It was five minutes after two when they reached home. The dinner dishes had been washed and put away, and Mother was sewing in the sitting room.

"I have to go home," said Anna. "Mother told me not to stay all the afternoon."

"I'll hitch up Ann Eliza," said Father. So he got out the Ford car and took the two girls and whirled them up the road three-quarters of a mile to Mr. Fowler's house. It was a pretty old white house with vines climbing over it, and flowers all around. Mrs. Fowler came out to greet them, with Bobby, who was Anna's four-year-old brother.

"Won't you come in?" asked Mrs. Fowler, who was a plump, busy woman, quite a little older than Louise's mother. She had a nutmeg grater and a nutmeg in her hand, for she had been making a custard pie when the car drove into the yard.

"No, I have a lot to do," said Mr. Martin. "The garden keeps me jumping, these days, what with the rain and the hot sun. The weeds grow a foot tall overnight."

"Yes, don't they?" said Mrs. Fowler. "Louise must come up and play with Anna. "You'll bring her up, won't you?"

"Surely I will. But we like to have Anna come to our house, and Louise's mother likes to know where she is. Well, young man, why don't you come to see us?" he said to Bobby, a round-faced little boy with yellow curls standing out all over his head.

"I'm comin'," said Bobby, "and I want to see chickies and cat. Anna must take me."

"Anna will." Mr. Martin started the car,

and he and Louella-Puella were at home almost
before they knew it. When Ann Eliza was
safe in the barn again ("Don't kick your stall
down," said Father, "and don't chew the
manger"), they still had the afternoon before
them. Father worked long and hard, weeding
the onions and the feathery little carrots, and
the cucumber vines, and tying up the beans
and tomatoes to the stout sticks which he had
cut. It was a great moment when the red
and brown bird was set up. It was nailed
securely to the top of a tall stick, and it sat
with its bright head held high, as if it were
very proud to be "the Queen of the Garden"
as Father called it. Mother had to come and
see, and praise the bird and the bird-maker,
and exclaim over the way in which the garden
things were growing. And then she went back
into the house, singing a little song. Father
went on with his weeding.

"Ah, here's a caterpillar!" he said, breaking off a leafy stem of a weed. "Come and
look at it, Pet."

Louise ran to look at the strange, hairy
creature dressed in orange and black. "Isn't

he an odd thing, Father?" she said. "He's
a little like a cat, isn't he? But I don't think
I'd want him instead of Flora."

"Let's see. I've thought of a verse," said
Father, who was always making up poems for
Louise. "How do you like this?

THE CATERPILLAR
"He's like a dear, soft pussycat:
   I should not care for him myself,
But what a woolly, snuggly pet
   He'd make, for some nice little elf!"

"Oh, I like that," said Louise. "He'd be a
lovely cuddle-cat for a fairy. Make me some
more verses, Daddy."

"Mm-m, let me think," said Father, pulling
at the weeds. "I'll make you some about crayfish—that's another word for crabs, you know.
They're about the crabs that you had in your
aquarium." He muttered a few minutes to
himself, and Louise knew he was making up
the verses as he went along. Then he recited
them for her:

CRAYFISH
"Down in the water you scuttle about,
   Over the pebbles and sand;

Out in the middle and close to the shore,
Where the blue irises stand.

"Queer little crayfish with pincers for claws,
I've a good feeling for you.
Don't be alarmed if a big little girl
Asks you a question or two.

"Where are your children? And wouldn't you
like
Crawling up here on the land?
And why do you always walk backward, my
dears,
Over the pebbles and sand?"

"I'll learn the poem and say it to the crayfish the next time I see any," said Louise. "You'll write it out on the typewriter, won't you, Father?"

"Yes, of course. And that's all for to-day, thanking you for your kind attention," said Father. "Hadn't you better go in and rest a while, Honey? I think Mother would like to see you."

Louise went into the house, and found that Mother was just finishing the work of mending a pinafore that Little Girl had torn a

few days before. They went upstairs to hang
it in Louise's closet, and to get the favorite
doll, Rosabelle.

When they were in Louise's room, Mother
stood looking around. "I do wish you had
a prettier room," she said. It was a pleasant
room, in itself, at the front of the house,
across the landing from Mother's. It had
two windows. From the front one you could
see away down over the hill and through the
village and across the creek and on into the
long fields beyond the town. You could even
see the lake which the stream ran into, though
from below it was shut off by trees. At the
other window you could look into the branches
of a cherry tree, and through them at the
side yard and the barn and the trees and
hills.

But the wall paper wasn't pretty. It was
full of curlicues and greenish blobs, with reddish lines running out from them. "I don't
understand how any one could have chosen
such paper," Mother grumbled. "The people
who lived here before were as neat and clean
as pins, but they surely didn't have much

taste." Some of the things in the room had been bought from the same people, because Father and Mother hadn't much furniture or much money, and were in a hurry to get settled. "There's been so much to do, and so much to buy, that we just couldn't get around to everything," said Mother. "But I can't wait any longer. We must do something to this room before the strawberries come on, or Father will be too busy to help."

They went downstairs and when Father came in to get a drink of water, Mother said, "Gordon, we must do something to Louise's room, before we do anything else. It's—well, it just *isn't pretty.*"

"I know it," said Father, looking distressed. "If I had my way, my Girl should have a room all ivory and seashell pink, with gold-framed looking-glasses and velvet carpets and silk cushions, and lace and swan's-down all over the bed."

"Oh, Gordon, what a room!" laughed Mother.

Louise laughed too. "It would be just like a fairy tale," she said. "But I don't believe

I'd want to stay in a room like that so very long.''

Father looked surprised. ''Wouldn't you? Dear me, I'm disappointed. I was going to have yours all fixed up like that, this very afternoon. Well, I'll have to tell the Fairy Godmother not to come, but it's too bad.''

Mother smiled at Louise. They were used to Father's ways. ''Seriously, now, Gordon ——'' she began.

''Seriously,'' he answered, ''there's that little check that I got for the children's verses that were taken last week. Why shouldn't we use that money to make Little Girl's room look better? We can put some new paper on the wall——''

''That's the chief thing,'' said Mother quickly.

''And I can paint the furniture any color you want,'' Father went on; ''sky-blue-pink or green-and-orange——''

''Horrors!'' cried Mother.

''And you can make new curtains and cushions and things with roses and birds on them——''

"Oh, I'd like that!" put in Louise.

"And it will cost hardly anything, but it will make a nicer nest for our Little Bird. I'll take you to town to get the paper and other things, to-morrow afternoon, if you like."

"I do like," Mother replied. "That will be splendid; and in the meantime I'll have to think hard and decide what would be right to have, without spending too much money."

So there was something new to think about, as well as another day of happy adventures to look forward to.

CHAPTER IV

PLAY AND PAINTING

Whooping and waving their arms, just because they felt so happy, the two little girls dashed up the hill behind the house. There was the orchard, where four or five rows of twisted old trees stood with thick grass growing around them. Under the last tree, the one highest up the hill, there was a sandy spot where the rain had washed down, and not much grass would grow. This was the place in which the girls had planned to build the kitchen of their house, because they could make a stove there. The parlor and the dining room and the bedrooms could go under the next trees, where there was plenty of grass to sit on and to use for carpets.

They had marked off the corners of the "best" room, before school was out, and had laid it off with stones and sticks and branches

to represent walls. In the parlor there was
even a sofa, made by putting a board across
two stones; and a table which Anna had made
with much labor, by pounding four sticks into
the ground and putting over them the round
wooden top of a barrel. It was rather "jog-
gly," as Louise said, but it was a wonderful
table, just the same. This morning Anna had
brought a table cover made from a flour sack
ripped open. She spread it out on the table,
and put in the middle a pickle bottle with two
red day lilies in it. It certainly did make a
handsome bit of furnishing for the parlor, and
even Flora was pleased with it. She jumped
up on the table to smell of the bottle and the
flowers, but Anna snatched her off and held
her in her arms. "No cats on our table," she
said sternly. But she kissed Flora on the soft,
clean white spot just between her ears. "Go
and climb the apple tree," she said, putting
Flora down on the ground at the foot of a
tree. Flora climbed up to the lowest limb,
and sat there looking up at the branches,
where a little bird was sunning himself. The
bird flew away, and Flora settled down on

the branch and watched the girls at their work.

"Now for the stove," said Anna. She had been thinking about that stove for nearly a week.

First a hole had to be dug in the sandy spot. "Father says we mustn't get it right under a branch, so that the fire will spoil the tree," said Louella. The ground was hard, and digging was not an easy task. They dug with a shingle and a broken bowl. Their hands were as black as the soil, but they did not mind. There were several trips to be taken to the rubbish pile near the barn in search of old bricks. Anna laid two bricks at the bottom of the hole which they had dug, and set two lengthwise at each side. This made a fire box in which the fire was safe from falling dirt. Next, two bricks were placed flat on the ground, on each side of the hole, to support the piece of tin which was to be the top of the stove.

The piece of tile which had been left when Father built a drain for the kitchen sink was about a foot long. How were they going to fasten it to the stove so that it would serve as a chimney? Louise was not of much use in this problem, but to Anna it had the joy of playing a game. She took two half bricks and put them a few inches apart at the back of the stove; then she set the tile up on them so that there was a good opening between them for the smoke to pass through. Now the flat piece of tin was put on, to make the smooth top of the stove where the cooking was to be done.

Anna stood off and looked at the stove. "It seems all right," she said, "but I s'pose we can't tell till we make the fire. Oh, I hope it won't smoke, except up the chimney!"

Louise, anxious to help, ran and got chips and kindling and a box of matches. "Mother says we must be very careful," she said when she came back. Hardly able to wait, Anna snatched the pieces of wood, and soon was lighting the fire in the fire box under ground. The smoke poured out through the tile, but it poured out all around it, too, and under the edges of the tin. It was clear that the stove was not a great success.

"We can't get at the fire, in front, and we can't keep the smoke where we want it," said Anna, half discouraged, but still eager to do something. "I wish I knew how to fix it."

"I'm sure I don't," said Louise. She would have been glad to do something else—play with dolls, or go for wintergreens, or swing in the barn—if Anna hadn't been so excited over the stove.

"Well, if it was like a real stove," said Anna, "it would have a place in front to get at the fire. I'm going to dig down a little, right here." She dug down, so that there was a little opening in front, where the air could go in, and where she could poke in some small sticks. "There! That's better!" The smoke went out at the back of the stove, now, and the fire burned more brightly. But Anna was still worried about the chimney. "The smoke should just go up the chimney; it shouldn't go up on both sides," she said, frowning. "I know what I'll do."

"What?" said Louise, getting interested. The cooking would be fun, if they ever came to it.

"Get some more tin, and use some dirt, and keep the smoke where it belongs." Anna ran and found some pieces of tin which had been left when the wall in the woodshed had been protected from the heat of the stove. She took these smaller pieces of tin and put them up close around the chimney, and then piled damp sand around the cracks. Then the smoke came out of the chimney just as it should do, and the fire blazed and crackled in the fire box lined with bricks.

Anna stood looking on, almost too proud to speak. "Oh, it's splendid. How did you know just what to do?" cried Louise. "The top of the stove is getting awfully hot. Just put your hand over it."

"We can cook things—real things," said Anna solemnly.

"Potatoes," suggested Louise.

"They take so long," objected Anna. "I can't wait."

"Bacon," said Louise.

"Do you suppose your mother'd let us?"

"Oh, I guess so. I'll see." Louise expected anything helpful from Mother. She ran down to the house, and came back with four strips of bacon on a plate, and two slices of bread, and a small frying pan. "Mother says we can keep this frying pan," she said excitedly. "It only cost ten cents, and we can keep it."

"Isn't she kind!" Anna could hardly believe such good fortune. "The bacon sandwiches were so nice yesterday, and now we have more to-day!"

It was wonderful to hear the bacon sizzling. "*Our own stove!*" said Anna. "We made it ourselves."

"You did most of it," said Louise honestly.

"It's ours, anyhow," said Anna. She had broken off a sharp stick, and was turning the bacon with it. Flora, smelling the savor, climbed down from her tree and came to sniff around the outdoor kitchen. How good the sandwiches were! "Cooking is the most fun," said Anna with her mouth full. "I could just cook all day, if any one would let me."

"I like the eating part, too," answered Louise with a giggle.

"Of course I do," said Anna; "but anyway I'd cook if some one else was to eat the things.

I guess I'll keep a boarding house when I grow up." Louise did not think that would be very much fun. She could think of a good many things nicer than that, but she did not say so. She fed Flora with a piece of her sandwich, and scattered a few crumbs for the ants.

Just then Father came up over the side of the hill. "Your mother said you were making a stove. I thought I'd come out and see it," he said. He hardly ever left his work in the forenoon, but once in a while he walked around the garden a little when he was having trouble with his writing. He was delighted with the stove. "You did well, Anna," he said. "I can help you a little, though. You wait." He went down to the woodshed, and came back with some gray mud in a basin. "This is cement or concrete," he said, showing the girls what he had. "It gets as hard as stone in a little while after it dries." He dug the sand away from around the chimney, cooled the pieces of tin, and then fitted them closely to the chimney, plastering them into place with the concrete, which he put on with a flat stick. He put sand over the outer edges. "There, now! you have a chimney that will hold the smoke all summer, if nothing happens. And I'll tell you what I'll do," he went on. "I'll make you a little two-sided roof, like a chicken coop, to put over your stove and keep it dry. You can take it off when you want to cook. How will that suit you?"

"That's just exactly what we need," said Anna, beaming with delight.

"I'd like to stay here and tinker with these things all day," said Father with a sigh, "but I've got to get back to my writing. I wish I had nothing to do but play."

"I think you like writing on your book," said Louise. "Maybe you like it as much as we like playing."

"Maybe I do," answered Father, stooping to smooth Flora's head. The kitty rose on her hind legs and rubbed her head along Father's hand, showing how much she liked to be noticed and loved.

Father went back to the house, and the girls went on with their playing. They found a box in the barn that would do for a cupboard

for their dishes (mostly broken ones) and for
their precious frying pan. Anna took a stone
and drove a nail into the inside wall of the
box, to hang the frying pan on, so that it
would be hidden and keep dry. It hardly
seemed any time until the forenoon was over,
and Anna had to go home.

In the afternoon, Father and Mother and
Little Girl went to town to get the things
which were needed to make Little Girl's room
look nicer. Mr. Rickman did not keep wall
paper and chintz in his store in Bellville.
Louise always liked the trip to the larger
town, five miles away. Ann Eliza could make
it in twenty minutes or less, but it was more
fun to drive slowly and look at things as you
went along. When they got to town, Louise
went with Mother to pick out the paper, but
after all she didn't have much to say about
it; for there were so many different kinds that
she couldn't choose any one of them. The
chintz was more exciting, for there were yards
and yards of flowers and birds and figures in
all sorts of colors and designs.

Mother took one kind, at last, that had some

lovely soft blue in it, and delicate, soft, rose-pink flowers with darker stems and leaves; and she bought other things, too, but Louise did not look at them, for she was interested in a case of beads and bracelets and bows of colored ribbon. Father bought cans of paint, and there were other parcels which were carried out and tucked away in the car. The most fun was when Father gave Louella three dimes, and told her that she might buy things at the ten-cent store for the playhouse in the orchard.

"I want to make them go just as far as I can," said Little Girl, holding up the three little silver pieces in her fingers.

"That's just the way I feel about my money," laughed Mother. "Come, let's see what we can get." It was Mother who knew that you could get cups for five cents if the saucers were missing, and odd saucers for five or three cents if the cups were missing. When the salesgirl found out that the dishes were going to be for a playhouse, she smiled, and brought out two pretty cups with bluebirds on them, and four saucers of different kinds (two of them had little nicks

along the edge that hardly showed), and sold
them to Louella for fifteen cents. Then there
was a basin that would do to cook in, and a
little saucepan with a handle, and the money
was all gone.

"It goes fast," said Little Girl, looking
rather surprised. "I thought it would last
longer."

Mother laughed. "It's just as well for you
to learn a little about money," she said, "and
how to be careful with it, without being afraid
to spend it. Are you satisfied, dear, with what
you've bought?"

"Yes, I guess so," said Little Girl, looking
at the rows and rows of wonderful things on
the shelves and counters; "but next time I'm
going to think it all over and decide what I
want, beforehand."

"That's the best thing to do," said Mother.
She had a list of the articles which she had
needed, and she was going through it to see if
she had forgotten anything. They met Father
at the newspaper office, where he had been
having some paper cut into the right size to
typewrite his book on; and they all got in

and started for home. (Louise did not say anything about ice-cream sodas, because she knew they cost a good deal, and she had already had the money for the playhouse dishes).

Almost as soon as they were at home, and had left Ann Eliza in the barn, Father put on the old clothes which he kept to wear in the garden, and he went up to Little Girl's room, and began to move out the furniture. "You'll have to sleep in the woodshed to-night," he said, "or out in the barn with Ann Eliza."

"Oh, dear," said Little Girl, "I don't believe I'll have to do anything like that. Where am I going to sleep, Mommy?"

"You'll sleep in the guest room," said Mother. They hardly ever had any guests, but there was a room for them, which did not look much nicer than Louella's. "That will be the next to claim attention."

When the furniture was all out of Louise's room, Father began tearing off the old paper. "This is one thing that I like to do," he said, as he tore off strip after strip of the ugly figured paper, "and I'm going to get it done to-day, so that I can do the painting to-morrow." Wherever the paper stuck to the plaster, he scraped it off with a knife; and he had some white powder that he called "plaster of Paris" that he mixed with water, to fill up nail holes and cracks with. It grew hard almost as soon as it was put into its place. Father carried the old paper out, to burn it in a sandy spot beyond the chicken yard, but Louise said, "Oh, Daddy, why don't we burn it after dark? It would make such a lovely bonfire."

"So it would," answered Father. "Well, after dark it is, then." He went back upstairs and put something that he called "sizing" on the wall with a brush. "It's made of glue and water," he explained, "and it's to make the paper stick tight to the wall, so that it will never come off." After that was done, Father had to go and work in the garden and let the chickens out, and do a dozen other things, and Louise stayed in the house and watched

Mother cutting off and hemming lengths of chintz, and making cushion covers, and in a little while it was supper time.

After supper, Mother washed the dishes and Louise wiped them, and then they all went out to see the bonfire. Father and Louise brought some dry leaves and branches, to make a bigger blaze. The long flames streamed up into the quiet air and made high-spired towers. "It's like a little city of fiery steeples, isn't it?" said Little Girl; "only they don't stay the same for more than a minute."

"I'm glad to see the old wall paper go," said Mother. "Perhaps when it was put on, some one thought it was nice, and was glad and grateful to have it. I hope we'll like ours, too, and be grateful for it."

"I'm going to be," said Little Girl. "And I'm happy for everything that makes our home better and prettier, aren't you, Mummy?"

"Indeed I am," answered Mrs. Martin, with her arm around Louella's shoulder. "I want our home to be the best and kindest place that

any one could think of, so that people will be
happy in it, and take happiness outside with
them when they go.''

"It's always going to be just like that " said
Little Girl.

It seemed strange to be going to bed in the
guest room, but Louise was too sleepy to think
about it, and in a little while it was morning.

The work on the improvement of Little
Girl's room couldn't begin till afternoon, because Father had to do a certain number of
hours of writing (nothing must interfere with
that); and Mother had her work to do, too,
and her shopping for Sunday.

After the morning's housework was done,
Mother put on her black hat with the blue
ribbon on it that she had worn a long time,
and Louise didn't put on a hat, and they took
a market basket and walked down around the
back of Mr. Quint's land and along the short,
narrow side street to the main street. There
was Mr. Rickman's store, a long white building with a wide, uncovered porch out in
front. There were two big dusty windows.

Through one you could see the post-office part of the store, and through the other you could see tin pails and washboards and boxes of oat-meal and bright-colored cans with salmon and soup in them.

The mail hadn't come yet—it didn't come till afternoon—and so the Martins' box was empty. Mother bought some stamps, and then at the other counter she bought the things she needed—sugar and butter and cheese and a great many other things, as well as a box of sardines for sandwiches, because Little Girl liked them so well. Mr. Rickman, a stout, good-natured man, patted Louise on the head and gave her a bag of peanuts. He had a boy, but no girls, and he was always especially nice to little girls. Eddie Rickman was in the store, wearing a checked shirt and blue over-alls—not dressed up in his suit, as he was when he went to school.

"Hello," said Eddie to Louise.

"Hello," answered Little Girl.

"Havin' a good time since school was out?" asked Eddie.

"Oh, just a fine time," said Louise.

"I been down to Pine River," said Eddie proudly. "I went to see my uncle 'n' aunt."

"That's nice," Louise replied. She wished she had an uncle and aunt who lived as near as Pine River, ten miles away. A little girl cousin would be a pleasant possession, too; but anyhow, there was Anna, and she was as good as any cousin to play with.

"I'm goin' to town on the Fourth," Eddie went on, "and we're goin' to have fireworks here in the evenin'."

"How splendid!" cried Louise. She had been wanting to know about that.

When she and her mother went home, they walked past the mill. They were going the long way round, because Mother wanted to stop at Mrs. Colter's and get a cross-stitch pattern to put on one of Little Girl's aprons.

The mill was a big, old, red building, three stories high in front and four at the back, because it was built on the high bank of the river. There was a high platform out in front, so that the farmers could easily unload the sacks of grain which they brought to be ground. The mill did not make white flour any more, as it had done in the old days, but it ground all kinds of feed for cattle, and corn meal, and buckwheat flour which could be used in making griddle cakes.

The old miller was standing up on the high platform. He wore a soiled white jacket and he was covered with a white, floury dust, even to his hat and his eyebrows, so that he looked like a dough man dipped in flour. He was a Welshman, it seemed, though Louise hardly knew what that was.

"Good day, Mr. Davids," said Mother.

"Good day, ma'am," answered Mr. Davids. "It's a fine warm day, ma'am."

"It surely is," said Mother.

"How's Miss Loo-eye-sy?" asked Mr. Davids.

"I'm well," said Louise. She liked Mr. Davids, but she did not know him very well, and she was a little afraid of him.

"Have you seen my mill?" he asked her.

"No, sir, I never have," said Louise.

"Would you like to see it?" he said, looking down at her rather fiercely from under his white eyebrows.

"Oh, I'd just love to," said Louise.

The old man smiled widely. "I'll tell you what," he said. "I'll give a party, a mill party. You can come and bring two or three other youngsters, and I'll show you the mill."

"Oh, that would be splendid!" said Louise, hopping up and down. "When, Mr. Davids? When will it be?"

"One day next week," said Mr. Davids, pleased with his own idea. "I'll have to ask my wife what day she wants it, and then I'll let you know."

"Thank you ever so much." Louise always tried to be polite. She walked on with Mother, or rather, Mother walked, and Louise skipped all the way to Mrs. Colter's.

In the afternoon, Father painted the woodwork in Louise's room. It had been white, but it was yellowed and dull and marred. Now he gave it a coat of fresh, creamy white. And not only that, but he let Louise paint. "I've just thought of something," he said. "I'm going to build a little bookcase under this window, for your books and magazines. I think

I can make it pretty quickly out of a box. And I'm going to let you paint while I'm tinkering.''

Nobody who has never painted knows how much fun it is to dip the brush in the thick, smooth paint, lift it quickly, so that it won't dribble, and then slap it up and down the woodwork like a real professional painter. It was a pleasure different from any other that Louise had known. She would have painted all the afternoon if Father had let her. It was a good thing that he had put down some newspapers, for the paint would dribble a little in spite of everything, and it looked streaky in some places. ''But I can fix that up with a stroke or two,'' said Father, ''and we'll burn the papers, and nobody will be the wiser.'' So Louella painted and painted, on the doors and the window sills and the mop board. She was sorry when Father had finished the bookcase and wanted the brush so that he might paint it. And when that was done, he went on with the painting, so fast that it was soon finished. The slowest work was painting the crossbars in the frames of

the windows, for the panes of glass were so
small that there were a good many. While
he was painting the window frames, Father
sang in a loud voice:

"I'm a peddler,
I'm a peddler,
I'm a peddler from Connecticut."

"What's the rest of the song, Father?"
asked Louise. She thought it sounded interesting.

"I've forgotten the rest," said Father, "but
anyway:

"I'm a peddler,
I'm a peddler,
I'm a peddler from Connecticut."

"I wish I knew what you sell," said Louise.

"Whew! it's hot to-day," said Father.
"What do you say, Pet? Shall we go in
swimming?"

"Oh, I'd love to," cried Louise. "Have you
done all you can here, and can we go right
away?"

"I've done all I can until the paint dries.
When the paper is on, the room will look

like the queen's bower. But it's too bad
that we have to leave it over Sunday.'' Father
was gathering up his painting materials and
the papers which had protected the floor. ''No,
we can't go right away, because I have plenty
of things to do, but a little before five o'clock
we can go.''

At a quarter of five, they were ready for
their swim. Mother said she would stay at
home and lie down, because she was warm and
tired. So Louise and her father went by
themselves. Louise had on her pretty blue
bathing suit which she had had the year before,
and over it was a little yellow oilskin cape.

Father had on his bathing suit with a raincoat over it. They ran down the back way to
Mr. Rickman's store, and then behind the
store to the pool and the creek below the mill.
Louise took off her cape, and Father threw
off his raincoat. ''In you go!'' shouted
Father. He whirled Louise off her feet and
bounced her into the water.

''Oo-oo!'' Louise shivered at first. The
water seemed cool, but it wasn't really cold.
In a minute it felt warm and comfortable.

The sand was soft under her feet. She and Father splashed each other as hard as they could, and Louise got the most water on her, because Father's hands were bigger than hers, and his arms were longer. She plumped down so that the water was up over her shoulders; but it was too shallow for Father.

"I'm going out where it's deeper," he said. "Come on. Swim, froggy, swim." He held his hands under Louise so that she couldn't go down, and showed her how to make her arms go for swimming. "That's right. That's good," he said, and before she knew it she was swimming along, and Father wasn't even holding her. But when she began to think about herself, she became confused and missed her stroke and began to sink; then Father was there again, holding her up. Last summer she had only waded and splashed, and had not learned to swim. Now she was actually learning.

The water was roaring down in a white waterfall from the flume beside the mill. "We'll climb up on the shelf below the falls," said Father. There was a wide wooden platform where the water fell down. It hardly showed because some of it was under water. Father helped Louise to swim over the deep black place, and then pushed and pulled her up on the platform, where the roaring water came down in a white wall, sending out a fine white spray. Father's arm was around her, and she was wet with the spray, and thrilled with the noise of the pouring falls.

"We're just like two ducks, sitting here, aren't we?" she said, laughing.

"Yes, a big one and a little one," Father answered. "Quack, quack," he said in a deep voice away down in his throat.

"Quack, quack," said the Duckling in a high, shrill voice.

Then Father sang, making up his song as he went:

> "Quack, quack, quack,
> There's water on my back.
> I think it is such luck
> That I'm a downy duck:
> The water doesn't stay,
> But dribble-drips away,
> And so I do not mind
> The waterfall behind.

Quack, quack, quack,
There's water on my back."

"Now what do we do next?" said the Duckling.

"Off you go!" said Father, and he pulled her off the platform, squealing a little, and they plunged into the dark pool. "Now we're seals. Yap, yap!" The seals swam about for a while. "Now we're sea lions. Ow-row-row!" Father was roaring like a sea lion and blowing out water from his lips. Then he sang another song:

"Oh, I'm a big sea lion bold,
I'm full of fish as I can hold.
I swim around and ramp and roar,
And gather fishes by the score.
Ow-row-row!

"I have a little lion child,
I drag her to the waters wild.
In waters down behind the store,
I teach her how to ramp and roar.
Ow-row-row!

"Roar, lion child, roar," he called.

She roared, with an "Ow-row-row!" But she laughed so that her mouth was full of water, and she was sputtering and coughing. "Oh, Father!" she cried, "what a funny father you are!"

"Don't you like my songs, Louella?" asked Father, looking injured.

"Yes, I do," said Louella.

"Then you shouldn't laugh at them. You'll hurt your poor old father's feelings." Louella laughed more than ever at this. "Now that you've laughed at me, you'll have to go home," said Father. But Louella knew that it was time to go home, anyway. "Out you go." He took her in his arms and swung her to the grassy bank. "Did you have a good swim?" He wrapped her in her little cape.

"Oh, a lovely swim, Daddy," said Louella. "What are we now, when we aren't sea lions?"

"We're storks," said Father. "Stretch your legs out, and walk like a stork.

"Here we go,
  Two storks in a row.
    Our necks are long,
    Our legs are strong (Now we make our
      necks and legs go),

Our eyes are bright,
Our wings are light (Now we flap our
    wings),
    And soon we'll fly
    Up in the sky.
So here we go—
Two storks in a row.''

Flapping their wings and lifting their legs high, the two storks made their way up the bank. ''Now we'll have to be folks,'' said Father, ''because we're coming back where the other folks are.''

''Oh, dear,'' sighed Louella, ''that isn't any fun.''

''We can't always be ducks and sea lions and such things,'' said Father. ''Life is real, life is earnest. Besides, Mother'll have something for us to eat, pretty soon, and I don't believe she has any stork food on hand at present, or sea-lion food, either.''

''Well, all right. I'll be a folk, then,'' said Louella. She and her father scampered past the store, and up the hill toward home.

CHAPTER V

Sunday was different from the other days. Father wasn't working, and they all went to church, and Louise stayed for Sunday school. When she got back, Mother was setting the table in the sitting room for dinner. "I never thought I'd do such a thing as eat in the kitchen," she was saying, "but our kitchen is such a nice place. The three windows make it so bright and cheery. And the yellow floor and the buff walls and the gingham curtains and the rag rugs are so sort of clean looking and interesting that I'm sure we all enjoy sitting down to eat in a place like that. And the screen shuts off the stove and the sink." Father had made a big folding screen which could be used to hide the part of the kitchen that was cluttered with cooking. "But just the same," Mother went on, "I like to have dinner in the sitting room a part of the time, so that we shan't get to be too careless and common."

Louise hardly knew what she meant, for Mother was always very particular to have everything on the table as neat and clean and pretty as could be.

"Let's eat in three different places to-day," said Father. "We had breakfast in the kitchen, and we're having dinner here, and let's have supper out under the apple trees, on the grass."

"Oh, yes! Let's do that," said Mother.

In the afternoon, Louise read in her books, which she had hardly looked at all the week, because she had been so busy, and Mother read her some stories out of the Bible. When supper time came, she helped Mother to make the sandwiches for the picnic in the orchard— sardine sandwiches, and cream-cheese sandwiches, and peanut-butter sandwiches.

Father wheeled the dishes out to the picnic place in a wheelbarrow. "I think these dishes ought to have a ride," he said. "Why, I don't suppose they've had a ride in ever so long, do you?''

''No,'' answered Louise, ''and I don't suppose they know the difference, either.''

''You don't?'' said Father, much surprised. ''Why, you know the difference when you have a ride, don't you?''

''Yes,'' said Louise, a little annoyed at the question; ''but I'm not a dish.''

''That's true,'' said Father, looking at her carefully. ''I believe you aren't. On the whole, I'm glad you're not a dish, because if you were, you'd have to sit on the shelf all the time.'' Then he began to sing:

''Hey, diddle, diddle, the cat and the fiddle,
The dish ran away with the spoon!''

He made the wheelbarrow go very fast up the grassy slope to the apple trees, and Louise had to run to keep up with him. When he stopped, little thin voices seemed to come from the dishes. ''Thank you, Mr. Martin,'' they said. ''Thank you for the ride.''

''There!'' said Father, turning to Little Girl, ''what did I tell you? They did like the ride, and they wanted an outing.''

"We were dreadfully tired of staying in the house," said the dishes, while Little Girl giggled.

"Well, well," said Tall Father, "I'm sure it must be dull. Louella-Puella will give you a ride every Sunday, and maybe once or twice during the week."

"Oh, that will be fun!" cried the dishes.

"No, no," said Louella, stamping her foot, "I don't want to do that. I can't bother. I haven't time."

"Why, how unkind you are!" said Father. "These poor dishes hardly ever get out, and surely you have all the time there is."

"Dear me," said Mother, who had come up with a plate of sandwiches and a thermos bottle, "what are you two talking about? I thought you'd have the tablecloth down, and the dishes set out."

Louella and Father scrambled to put the tablecloth on the grass. It was all in waves and bumps, where the grass and weeds held it up. Flora ran under the edge of the cloth and scratched and played till she tipped over the bottle of olives, and bounced the cake off

its plate. So she had to be pulled out from
under the cloth and amused with a little green
apple tied to a stick.

It was a delightful picnic, and it lasted a
long time. They all stopped to listen to the
robins singing, and to play with Flora, and
to look off down the hill, past the house and
past Mr. Quint's land, and Mr. Rickman's
store (they could just see the roof), to the
lake and the marsh and the fields beyond the
town. Once a whole flock of crows flew overhead, cawing and making a loud outcry, and
Father repeated some verses he had made for
Louella:

"At sunset, when the sky is red,
  The crows go flying overhead,
  Like small black airships, sailing high,
  And 'Caw, caw, caw!' they loudly cry.
  They're coming home from near and far,
  To where their wives and children are.
  It's nice for them, but when they call
  'Caw, caw,' I am not pleased at all;
  For when the crows fly overhead,
  I know it's nearly time for bed."

After the supper had been cleared away, and
the dishes packed into the wheelbarrow again,

Father took a little book out of his pocket, and read poetry to Mother. It was a book called *The Earthly Paradise,* full of long, strange, musical stories, which Little Girl only partly understood; but she couldn't help listening, because the lines sounded so beautiful. She sat so still that Flora gave up waiting for her, and went hop-hopping like a rabbit through the tall grass.

On Monday morning, the paint in Louise's room was dry, and Father said he would put on the paper in the afternoon. Louise helped her mother with the breakfast things and with the feeding of the chickens; and then Anna came, with her little brother Bobby, and there was great fun, playing with the stove and the playhouse in the orchard.

Anna brought three tin forks, which her mother had given her for the playhouse; and some cold boiled potatoes with butter for frying them in the little frying pan; and buttered biscuits with thin slices of ham between. She was more pleased than Louise herself with the dishes from the ten-cent store. "Aren't

they perfectly grand?'' she said, lifting them
and looking at them on all sides. ''Now we
don't have to play with broken ones, and it
seems more like real housekeeping. Mamma
says maybe she can find something on the
top shelf of the pantry, when she gets time
to look—some saucers and jars and things.''

Bobby sat down to make sand houses, piling
the fresh sand over his bare foot to form a
door. The girls busied themselves with their
house and the wonderful stove. At half past
ten, the three children had their lunch of
potatoes and biscuits, and a sardine apiece, left
over from last night's sandwiches.

The most exciting thing, because it was
something new, was watching the work of
papering the wall in the freshly painted room
upstairs. Mother had made the paste out of
flour and water, boiled till the mixture looked
like a cornstarch pudding. Father laid some
boards across two chairs, to make a pasting
table, and he brought up some scissors and
some clean cloths. Mother, in her biggest
apron, was there to help him. It seemed amaz-
ing, to Louise, to see them cutting the paper

and pasting the back of it, and then very carefully fitting it into place on the wall, and smoothing it down with a cloth. "It's wrinkly in some places," said Louise, feeling worried lest the pretty paper should not be right when it was really on the wall.

"It will be smooth when it gets dry," said Father. "It contracts, you know, when it dries—that is, it draws tighter, and the wrinkles smooth themselves out." Father was too busy even to sing, while he was at the task of papering. He held his lips tight together, and his forehead was puckered as it was sometimes when he was writing. Mother helped with the handling of the strips of paper, but Father stood on a box and put them where they belonged.

Flora jumped up on the board table and put her pink tongue into the paste, and almost stepped on the pasted strip of paper. Louise pulled her off just in time.

When the paper was all on, you wouldn't have known the room—it looked so large and fresh and attractive. The paper was a light creamy color, with small pale bunches of flowers on it, so faint that it was almost like a plain paper, only more interesting. The floor had to be painted, and so it was another day before everything could be finished.

At last the time came when the room could be put in order for Little Girl to sleep in again. Mother put up the new curtains of dotted muslin, ruffled and looped back. Then she made a dressing table by taking a small cheap table that she had, and tacking on a flounce of the chintz with the lovely blue and rose figures in it. Over the dressing table she hung a looking-glass with its frame painted dull blue. The rugs came out of the guest room. They were hand-woven ones, of gray and tan rags, with touches of blue in them.

On the other side of the room was the shabby pine chest of drawers which had been in the room before, but Father had painted it a soft tan (with lines of blue, and blue knobs)—''So that we'll have some warm color in the room,'' said Mother. ''Blue is a cold color, you know.'' Louise didn't know, but she liked to hear about it. The small maple bedstead was a warm color, too, with the yellow tones of the old wood. The willow chair and the low wooden chair had cushions of the chintz. The low, strong table beside the window was given a cloth cover of tan, with a blue edge. Here Louise was to keep any books that she happened to be reading, and her water-color paints, and her sewing basket, and a vase of flowers. Mother put a jar of pink roses and bluebells on the table, and another on the chest of drawers, and she hung up two pictures which Little Girl especially liked. One was "The Strawberry Girl," by Sir Joshua Reynolds, and the other was a Japanese print of small brown birds on a branch, against a yellow sky. Louise was happy in putting her own books into the shelves which Father had made for them, under the window; and she helped Mother to make the long cushion that went on the top of the window-seat bookcase, where she could sit and read. It was a "sweet room," as Mother said, and a "bower for our Bird," as Father called it. Louise could hardly stay out of it the first day that it was finished, and Father was almost as fond of staying in it as she was. Before she went to bed, he came up and sat in the willow chair, and held her on his lap, and told her stories. She put her arms around his neck and said, "Thank you, thank you, Tall Father, for my nice new room."

Father said, "We love to have you in it, dear, and the thanks for the room belong mostly to Mother."

Mother came into the room just then, and she said, "You know you did most of the work, Gordon."

And Father answered, "But you did most of the thinking, and the thinking is the first and most important thing."

Louise put her arms around her mother's neck and said, "Thank you, dear Mother, for the nice, nice new room." And then it was time to go to bed. She lay sniffing the fresh, painty smell, and watching the shadows get darker on the flowered wall and the blue-framed looking-glass, and feeling quiet and joyful because she had such a pretty nest, all her own; and then she was asleep and dreaming about playhouses and Pussy Flora.

Mr. Davids had sent word that the mill party was to be on Thursday. Louise and Anna and Bobby were invited, and Eddie Rickman and Amy Colter, besides. On Thursday afternoon, a little before three, they all met at Louise's home, and went down together to the mill. Louise wore her blue linen frock and her white hat with the daisies on it. She hardly ever wore a hat in the summer, except when she went to church, and so she felt especially dressed-up and "partified" at this time. Anna had a pink gingham dress, which looked nice with her dark hair and brown eyes. Bobby wore his short dark blue trousers, buttoned to a white tucked waist. His round cheeks were red with excitement and pride at being asked to a party with older boys and girls. Eddie and Amy were dressed in their best clothes.

When they arrived at the mill, Mr. Davids was waiting for them on the top of the steps leading to the high platform in front of the mill. He had on clean blue overalls and a fresh white jacket, but his eyebrows and his short, stiff beard seemed as floury as ever.

"Here you are," he called out in a loud voice when he saw the group of children coming. He took Bobby and swung him to the platform. "Up you go!" he cried, and then he swung the three girls up, leaving Eddie to walk up in the usual way. "Janie," he called to his wife, who was inside the mill, "here's our party!"

Then there was Mrs. Davids at the door, a stout, elderly woman in a black-and-white dress and a starched apron. She kissed Bobby and the girls, and patted Eddie on the shoulder. "Well, well, here you are," she said. "Now, Husband's going to show you the mill, and I'll stay here, because I don't like climbing up and down stairs."

Louise and Anna giggled a little at her calling Mr. Davids "Husband." "But he is," whispered Anna, "and why shouldn't she call him that?"

"Nobody else does," whispered Louise, giggling again, when she thought of Mother's speaking of Father in that way.

"We'll go around and have a look at the mill," Mr. Davids was saying, "and then maybe there'll be something to nibble on. Do you think you could crunch an ear of corn, or chew a handful of oats?''

The children looked rather frightened. "I— I don't know," stammered Louise, who felt that somebody must say something in order to be polite. "I don't think we ever tried."

"So?" said Mr. Davids. "Well, maybe there'll be something better than that." He winked one eye very slowly and looked over at his wife.

Mrs. Davids smiled and nodded at the children. "He's just teasing you," she said. "Don't worry. You won't have to eat corn."

Louise was thinking that probably Mr. Davids was a "teasing man" like Tall Father, who often talked in such a queer way that you couldn't tell whether he were making fun or not.

"Come on," said Mr. Davids. "Down cellar first. My son Toby is making the mill go, while I'm a guide for the party." They all climbed down some stairs, where only a little light came through small, floury windows. They found themselves in a big cellar with stone walls and stone posts. There were dark corners hung with cobwebs, and nooks where old lumber was piled. On the lighter side of the cellar there was some machinery, with iron bars and wheels. From an open window, the children could see the big waterwheel. "That's where the water comes down out of the flume, and turns the wheel, and makes everything go," explained Mr. Davids. The rushing of the water and the creaking of the wheel made an echoing noise, so that it was hard to make oneself heard above the din. There was a shaking and trembling, too, and a kind of low roar which seemed to come from upstairs, where the millstones were grinding the grain.

"It's like a giant's cavern," said Louise.

"Huh," said Eddie. "It's just a mill."

Louise could almost imagine a giant stalking out of the shadows, but she was not afraid; for she thought he would be a good giant, though perhaps a teasing one, like Father or Mr. Davids.

"Now we'll go back upstairs," said the miller. They went up again to the floor which they had been on before. He showed them the hoppers, where the grain was sliding down upon the white, mealy stones, which were going slowly round and round. There was a warm, close smell of machinery and grain, and of brimstone or matches, and that was the smell which the stones made, grinding against each other. When the children looked up, they saw long, square, wooden pipes coming down out of the ceiling, and the grain was dripping down through these pipes and falling little by little into the hoppers. It all seemed very strange and mysterious. "Keep away from the machinery," said Mr. Davids. "Don't go too near." Anna kept tight hold of Bobby's hand, and Amy Colter was pulling at Louise's sleeve. Eddie went up as close as he dared to everything, and pretended that he was going to touch the big white moving millstones, so that Mr. Davids had to call to him, "Look out!"

In the shed at the side of the main part of the mill, there was a corn sheller. Piles of yellow corn were going through a huge hopper, where the kernels were taken off, and the cobs were tossed aside. "Ha, ha!" laughed Mr. Davids, "these little ladies here thought they'd have to bite the corn right off the cob, just like that!" He patted them on the head. "Never mind. You won't have to eat that sort of stuff." Louise couldn't help wondering what they were going to have to eat, but she kept her thoughts to herself.

"Come on, now," said the miller, "and I'll give you a ride on the truck."

The truck was not a wagon, but an "up-and-down wheelbarrow," as Anna called it, with two small wheels close to the floor. The rider stood up with his back to the handles, and his feet on the little shelf at the bottom (made for carrying bags of grain), and had a delicious bumpy ride over the rough boards of the floor. "Whoo-oo!" called Mr. Davids, as he wheeled Anna up and down the passageway between the hoppers. "Whoo-oo!" shouted all the rest as they ran along beside the truck. Anna could only laugh and hold on breathlessly to the sides of the truck, and even then she was almost bumped off.

"Me next, me next!" cried Bobby. Mr.

Davids wheeled him carefully, because he was not very good at holding on.

Louise came after Bobby. She could hardly keep from squealing with joy, as Mr. Davids, with his long "Whoo-oo!" pushed the little truck up and down the floor of the mill, and around the corner into the shed, where the corn sheller was working. The others ran whooping beside her, and she pretended that she was Queen Elizabeth being driven in her carriage through the streets of London, while the people crowded around, shouting, "Long live the Queen!" She knew that Anna would have laughed at such imaginings. "But I don't have to tell her," she thought, "and it's fun to pretend being a Queen."

After everybody had had a ride, the miller said, "Come on. There's more to see." So they all trooped up to the next floor. There were big bins on all sides, some of them empty, and some full of grain which Mr. Davids said was rye or oats. The children stopped to lift handfuls of it, letting it slide down through their fingers into the bin again. Some of the long, square troughs which they had seen downstairs, bringing the grain to the hoppers, ran from these bins. "More yet," said the guide, and they all climbed one more flight of stairs to the top story of the mill. "We don't use this now," said Mr. Davids. It had a deserted look, and the cobwebs seemed longer and more floury than down below. The bins were all empty and covered with dust. Swallows flew in and out of a broken window at the front, and fluttered among the rafters. The children ran back and forth, saying "Whoo-oo!" to each other, to hear their voices echo in the spaces under the roof. "Come here," said Mr. Davids, stepping to a window at the back. A pane of glass was gone, and he let each child stick his or her head out of the window to look around. Louise was surprised to see how far, far down the flume was, with the water rushing against the darkness where the waterwheel was hidden. On one side, she could see the meadow and the foundry where she and Anna loved to play. Farther over she could see a cow and some white geese. On the other side she could look almost at the spot where she and Father had had their swim, and where they had sat pretending that they were ducks, with the water from the flume spattering on their backs.

"Ain't that a pretty sight?" said Mr. Davids.

"Yes, it's lovely," answered Louise, bringing her head in. She wanted to look for a longer time, but she did not like to keep anybody waiting.

Last of all, Mr. Davids put his head out, and looked around like a turtle peering out of his shell. Louise was afraid that he would catch his ears or his whiskers, and not be able to get his head back in again; but after a little twisting, he succeeded in bringing it inside. "Well, now we tramp down," he said. "Make all the noise you want to. My wife don't care." So they clattered down the stairs like a band of war horses, and came bouncing into the open space at the front of the first floor, where Mrs. Davids was unpacking sandwiches from a basket.

"Mm-m," said Anna in Louise's ear. "Something to eat!"

"Well, dearies," said the miller's wife, smiling around at the eager young faces, "did you see everything?"

"Yes'm," they all answered at once, except that Louise said, "Yes, Mrs. Davids," as her mother had taught her to do.

"And did you like it?" asked Mrs. Davids, unwrapping a frosted cake.

"We thought it was wonderful," said Anna.

"It was terribly interesting," said Louise. All the children were staring at the cake. They saw that it had nuts and candies on the top.

"Husband, where's the lemonade?" said the lady, turning to Mr. Davids.

"It's in my office," said Mr. Davids, hurrying to get it. The office was a part of the mill which the children had not seen. Mr. Davids came back carrying a huge pail of lemonade with ice in it. Slices of lemon floated on the top, with the yellow rinds shining.

"I do hope it's sweet enough," said Mrs. Davids, looking anxious.

"I'm sure it is. I put in pounds of sugar,"

Mr. Davids said. He was setting up a folding table for the glasses and the sandwiches and the cake, and finding boxes and stools and overturned baskets for the children to sit on. Soon everybody was enjoying the lemonade (which *was* sweet enough) and the other good things as well. Toby, the miller's son, a heavy, red-cheeked young man, came and had some of the refreshments with them, and then hurried back to his grinding. When the big cake was cut, there was a candy heart on each piece, and little red wintergreen candies, and the halves of hickory nuts left over from last year. It was just the kind of cake that children especially like. There was plenty of lemonade, so that every one could have two or three glasses.

"I do love to have enough of everything," said Mrs. Davids, beaming about at them all. "And I want our mill party to be a success."

"It is a success," said Louise and Anna together.

Eddie took a long drink to cover up his shyness, and said, "It surely is." Louise knew that if he had not been trying to speak very properly, he would have said, "It sure is."

"When I was a boy, back in Wales," began Mr. Davids, "we didn't have things like this to eat and drink."

"Oh, tell us about it," said Louise quickly.

That was just what Mr. Davids wanted. He told them about the farm he had lived on, with its gray stone house and the hilly fields and stone walls and hedges; and about the fireplace in the kitchen, where the cooking was done, and the kind of food that was eaten. And he told them stories of the countryside, and of people who thought they had seen the "piskies" or pixies, in the fields, fairy folk that played mischievous pranks on boys and girls, or did unexpected deeds of kindness for them.

The little listeners were all so absorbed in what he was telling them that they forgot about going home. "Now this is all," he said at last. "I can't tell you any more."

"I think we'll have to be going," said Louise, beginning to be afraid that they had stayed too long to be polite.

"You haven't seen the office," said Mr.
Davids. There wasn't much there to see, except a rusty stove, and shelves for account
books, and an old desk at which one stood up
to write. And there was a chair with a red
cushion in it, and on the cushion a Maltese
cat was curled up, sound asleep.

Louise ran to give the kitty a hug, for she
could never resist a cat. "Oh, I wish I had
known about you before!" she whispered. The
cat stretched and yawned, and sniffed at Little Girl's hand, and then went back to sleep
again.

Mr. Davids was taking something out of the
desk (it had a lid that lifted up). "Here's
something for each of you," he said. He gave
them each a picture postcard with a picture
of the mill on it, taken from a photograph. It
showed the mill and the flume and the waterfall, with a glimpse of the shore and the trees,
and even the irises, and the white geese swimming about.

"Oh, thank you, thank you," said the boys
and girls. They all went back to the front of
the mill, and shook hands with Mrs. Davids

and said *Thank you* to her, and then shook
hands with Mr. Davids, and said good-by to
him.   Then they went out at the big floury
door, and the mill party was over.

CHAPTER VI

WHAT MOTHER WANTED

A few days later, Louise was walking along the path between the house and the barn. All at once she spied something red among the leaves of the strawberry bed. "A berry! a berry!" She swooped down into the bed, turned up the spreading leaves, and there was a ripe red strawberry, hanging heavily on its short stem. "I'll pick it for Mother," said Little Girl aloud; but just then she saw another, and another. "We can each have one," she went on. "I'll look and look, and be sure I get them all." When she had gone carefully over the whole bed, she had picked twelve. She piled them on a rhubarb leaf, and did not eat one, though her mouth was watering for the ripe crimson berries. "Four for each of us," she said, "not counting Flora."

Then she ran into the house, holding her leaf basket. Mother was in the kitchen, beating the whites of eggs, to make a tapioca pudding. "Look, Mother, look!" cried Little Girl.

"Well, I declare," said Mother. "The strawberries are really ripe." She was surprised and pleased, because it was rather early for the berries.

"There are four for you," said Little Girl. "Pick out the biggest."

"Oh, no," said Mother; "that wouldn't do. I'll shut my eyes and take them just as they come." So she shut her eyes and picked out four of the berries, and it turned out that one was the smallest of all. Little Girl wanted her to change it for a bigger one, but Mother laughed and said that we must all take what we get and not complain. "They're sweeter than the first ones usually are," she said as she ate them.

"Father must have his," said Little Girl. "Do you think I dare disturb him at his writing? This is so—so important, Mummy."

"Yes, it is important," Mother agreed. So many things depended on the strawberry crop

—Father's new suit, and Louise's shoes and fall coat, and Mother's silk dress that she needed so much, and the gasoline to keep Ann Eliza going. "You try," Mother encouraged Little Girl, "and see what he says."

Louise tiptoed into the sitting room and over to the door of Father's study. It was half closed. She tapped faintly on the door.

She heard her father say, "A woodpecker. I hear a woodpecker on the maple tree." She tapped again. "What a nuisance of a woodpecker," said Father. Then he repeated some verses that he had made for Louise. The poem was called "Mr. Woodpecker."

"His breast is speckled white and black,
  And stripes adorn his wings and back;
  His throat is gray, and on his head
  He wears a pretty cap of red.
  Among the leaves you see him fly,
  To our big maple, standing by;
  Then holding by his slender toes
  And tap-tap-tapping as he goes,
  He searches up and down the tree,
  In hopes to find a worm for tea."

Louise laughed out now. "It isn't a woodpecker, Father,'' she said. ''It's me. May I come in?''

''If you're white, stay out; if you're black, come in,'' called Father in a deep voice. This was a joke which he and Louise practiced on each other.

''I'm black,'' said Little Girl, pushing open the door. ''Just see what I have, Poppy. I couldn't wait to show you.''

''Good gracious!'' said Father, staring at the leaf basket and the eight ripe strawberries, ''what queer-looking red things. Where did you get those?''

''Out of our garden, of course,'' answered Louise. Sometimes Father was provoking.

''What are they?'' asked Father.

''They're strawberries,'' said Louise crossly.

Father kept on looking at them, and he let his mouth fall open, so that he seemed like a surprised little boy. He ran his hand through his hair, too, so that it stood up straight all over his head. ''Strawberries?'' he said. ''What are they? I don't see any straw.''

''Strawberries are—why, they're strawberries,'' said Little Girl.

"Who'd have thought it?" answered Father. "But what are they *for?*"

Louise hardly knew whether to laugh or cry. "They're to eat." She never seemed to know what to do when Father teased like that. "I found twelve, and that makes four apiece for us, not counting Flora."

Father opened his eyes wider. "How did you figure that all out?" he said, looking astonished and proud. "What a wonder-child you are at arithmetic! Now, let's see. You said there were twelve"—he counted on his fingers—"and there were how many of us, did you say? Three? Four? And how many did you say that would make for each of us? Really, I can't do such big sums. I'm glad you can, for then I don't have to."

Louise squealed. "Oh, Poppy, don't talk like that," she cried. "Let's eat 'em. I can't wait."

"You poor little thing." Father put his arm around Little Girl and hugged her up close to him. "Did her old father tease her? Well, well, it's too bad. Let's eat the strawberries.'' He laid them out on his desk. ''Here,'' he popped one into Louise's mouth, and then popped one into his own. ''Oh, they are good, aren't they?'' He sighed. ''It's fine to see them coming on, but it means a lot of work.'' They finished the strawberries, Father with his arm around Louise's shoulders. ''I hope we'll get a good crop. I don't see why we shouldn't. Here's a good crop of writing, anyhow.'' He lifted a large pile of papers, with typewriting on them.

''It's your book, isn't it?'' said Louise. It seemed queer that a book could be just a pile of papers. ''Is it finished?''

''Almost,'' answered Father.

''What are you going to do with it?''

''Send it away, and see if anybody will print it, Louella-Puella.''

''Why shouldn't they print it?'' asked Louella.

''Of course. Why shouldn't they?'' Father laughed, and then sighed again. ''I hope some one will. I've worked hard enough on it. Now, run on, Pet, and let me work. I want to get it done as soon as I can. Thank you

for the strawberries. You were a good girl
to bring them in.''

"You aren't cross because I bothered you?''

"No, not this time. Don't do it often,
though. I might get fierce.''

Louella went out slowly, because she
wanted to stay; but she knew that Father's
work was one of the most important things
that concerned the Martins. That, and the
strawberries and the other fruit and the garden were the means of making a living for
them all.

The days were going on swiftly now, as
they do after a vacation has really started.
Little Girl played by herself in the barn, and
pretended that Mrs. Periwinkle and Mrs.
Montgomery were calling on each other; and
she read her books all through again, and a
new one that Father sent for, and one that
Amy Colter lent her; she and Anna spent
hours in their playhouse in the orchard; and
she went to visit Anna, and they paddled and
splashed in the little brook that ran through
the field behind the barn. And Little Girl
helped her mother a good deal in the house,

and learned to sew carpet rags to make the woven rugs that Mother liked so well, and to take care of her pretty room in the neatest sort of way, and to do a great many other useful things.

"I want you to be interested in our house," said Mother, "and help to make it comfortable and pleasant to look at."

"I want to learn how," said Little Girl. So Mother showed her how to do things, and told her about the colors that go together and those that don't, and explained to her that certain kinds of furnishings "belong" in an old house, and certain kinds don't "harmonize" at all.

On the morning after the strawberries had first ripened, Mother had ironed the sitting-room curtains, and had just finished putting them up on their brass rods. "This is rather a nice room," said Mother, as she stepped back to see that the curtains were hanging properly. It was a good-sized square room, with windows only on one side, because the small parlor (or reception room, as Mother laughingly called it) was in front, and Father's study was at the side, and the kitchen was at the back. The two windows looked out toward the village and the long path that led through the yard and out to the barn.

"It's a nice room," said Mother, "or it would be if it only had a fireplace." The house had been built just at the time when people were beginning to think that fireplaces were old-fashioned. If Father could afford it, he was going to put in a pipeless furnace in the fall, and that would keep the house beautifully warm. The stoves had been a bother, the winter before. "A fireplace would be such a pleasure," Mother went on. "We could use it a great deal on cool evenings before we started the furnace, and in the spring, too. And it would even be a comfort in the winter, to make the house look cheerful on gloomy days."

Louise sat thinking. It surprised her a little to hear Mother saying that she *wished she could have something.* It seemed as if Mother never wished for things, and never complained because she didn't have as much as she had had at home before she was married. She just worked on quietly, and made everything as comfortable as she could for Father and Little Girl, and seemed to want to be with them rather than anywhere else. She could get along with ever so little if she only had them. And now Mother wanted a fireplace.

"Couldn't we have one put in?" asked Louise.

"Not very well," answered Mother. "It would cost a good deal, and we have to use the money for the furnace. Besides, it would be a terrible bother, tearing out the walls and building a new chimney. What we really need," she said, after a pause, "is a Franklin stove."

"What is a Franklin stove?" asked Louise.

"Why, it's something that Benjamin Franklin invented," Mother replied. "It's like a fireplace, only it's made of iron, and you can have a short pipe in it, that fits into a stove-pipe hole. You can burn wood or coal in it, just as you like."

"Is it right open, like a fireplace, so that you can see the fire?" asked Louise.

"Yes, it's open as wide as a fireplace, so

that you can look right at the fire,'' said
Mother, ''and make toast, and roast marsh-
mallows and chestnuts, and put in pine cones
and watch them burn. And a kitty cat like
Flora can snuggle up in front of it on the
rug, and go to sleep, and little girls can sit
down on a cushion before it and read their
books or sew their carpet rags or play with
dolls.''

''Oh, how lovely, Mother,'' said Louise.
''We *should* have one.''

''We could put one against that front wall,
there,'' said Mother, ''where the stove stood
last winter.'' She stood looking at the place
as if she saw the fire burning and crackling
in the Franklin stove. ''I know what I'll do,''
she went on. ''I'll buy one.''

''Can you, Mommy?'' cried Louise, jumping
up. ''Is there any place that you can get
one?''

''The old ones are the nicest,'' said Mother,
''that people have had in their families for
years and years. But I don't suppose I could
find an old one around here, and I know a
place where I could get a new one, made like

the old stoves. I think it would cost about sixty dollars.''

''Oh, goodness! that's a lot, isn't it?'' said Louise. It seemed like a huge fortune. She remembered how quickly the money went when she was buying anything at the ten-cent store. ''How are you going to get the money, Mother?''

Mother laughed. ''I'll find it rolling up hill in a barrel,'' she said. Then she explained. ''You know Grandma sends me a little now and then; and Mr. Rickman pays me for all the eggs that we don't use ourselves, and— and I think I'll go without the silk dress I was going to have when the strawberry money came in.''

''Oh, Mommy!'' Louise put her arm around Mother's waist. ''You mustn't go without that dress.''

''We'll see.'' Mother pressed a little light kiss on Louise's cheek. ''Now, don't tell Father anything about this, will you? It would worry him to know that there was something I wanted very much and couldn't have;

"I won't tell him unless I have to," said Louise. Mother hardly heard her, for she had gone to get a tape measure, to measure the space between the corner and the door that led into the front room.

Louise thought about the fireplace a good many times after that, but she did not say anything to Father. He was finishing his book, and getting the strawberry boxes and crates ready for the hurried work of the next few weeks.

It was now almost the end of June, and the Fourth of July would soon come and go. As Father said, it seemed, when the Fourth was over, that the summer was beginning to get short. On one of these late June days, Father sent off his book. That was the really important thing of the month, he said—next to Little Girl's beginning her vacation. He read the book all through to Mother, one afternoon and evening. Louise heard only scraps of it, because she and Anna and Eddie Rickman were swinging in the barn, and playing Pull-Away between the fence and the schoolhouse, and having other exciting times.

The next morning, Father wrapped the book up in many thicknesses of brown paper, and tied it securely, and wrote on the parcel the name of a publishing company in New York. Then he brought out Ann Eliza, and all the family (except Flora) got in, and rode to the town five miles away, and Father left the book at the express office, to be sent to the publishing company. Father and Mother both looked sober, and Father did not laugh or sing or make jokes. Louise found out that when you are sending away a book which you have worked a long time on, you feel relieved, but you feel anxious, too, and uncertain.

"Oh, I *hope* it will be taken," said Mother in a low voice, when Father was coming out of the express office.

"I hope so, too," answered Louise, though she was not quite clear as to what would happen if it were—or weren't.

Father stood looking at Mother, and forgetting to get into the car. "I wonder whether I ought to have changed that eighth chapter," he said with a wrinkle between his eyes. "Do you really think it ought to have been left as it was?"

"I think it was exactly right," said Mother. "If you fuss with a thing, you're so likely to spoil it. Now, Gordon, don't worry over places in that book that you think could be improved. You've done what you could on it, and you've sent it off, and there's no use in making yourself unhappy."

"I know it," said Father. "I'm going to forget about it for a while." He got into the car, but did not start it.

"Let's see," said Mother. "It will take about three days to get to New York, won't it?"

"Yes, but it will be weeks before we hear from it, I suppose," said Father. "Those big publishing houses take their time. They don't care how a poor, unheard-of chap out in the Middle West is feeling. Why, you know, Henry Trumbell waited six months when he sent in his book, and he wouldn't have heard then, if he hadn't——"

"Oh, come, Gordon," said Mother, "it won't be any six months. Don't get that idea in your mind. I think you'll hear in a very short time."

"But, Father," broke in Louise, who was tired and puzzled, "if the publishing folks do take it, what then?"

Father looked at Mother. "Fame and fortune," he said, laughing. "Maybe!"

"And what if they don't take it?" asked Louise.

Father stuck out his chin in a grim way, and started the car. "I guess we'll just have to try again, Pet," he said. "How about some ice-cream sundaes? This is an Event, you know, and we must celebrate." So they all went to the candy shop and had ice cream, and nothing more was said about the book.

That night there were three small dishes of strawberries for supper. The next day there were a few more. "I think we'll have a good many by the Fourth," said Mother. She had been looking at the bed near the house, where the berries ripened first, and at the two big beds out behind the house, beyond the orchard.

"Then our hard work begins," said Father.

The morning of the Fourth was cool and

clear. Louise was up early, for she had a good many bunches of firecrackers to shoot off, and she could hardly wait. Even before breakfast she was out, and Father was helping her.

Bang! bang! Fizz! fizz! At the first loud noise, Flora was off like mad on a run for the barn. *Bang! Bang! Bang!* Louise laughed to hear the uproar. Father laughed, too, but Mother looked as if she didn't enjoy it as much as "the two children," as she called Father and Louise. Father sang "Columbia, the Gem of the Ocean," at the top of his voice, while he was lighting the firecrackers, and Louise joined in at the ends of the lines.

"Breakfast, breakfast!" called Mother. "Come along, Little Ones. Everything will be cold."

There was a little silk flag on the table, in honor of the day. "We have corn-meal mush," Mother announced, "to remind us of what our ancestors in the Colonies had to eat, and how different their lives were from ours."

"I like it," said Louise. "But I don't suppose they had sugar and cream on it, do you?"

"No, I don't believe they did," answered Mother, "and there were a great many other things that they didn't have, either."

After breakfast, Louise made her bed and helped with the dishes and with the feeding of the chickens; and she and Father shot off more firecrackers, and after a while all the Martins changed their clothes and got into the car, and whirled away to the town five miles away, where there was to be a procession at eleven o'clock. There were dozens of cars on the road, each one loaded with gayly dressed people, and even babies and dogs. The Fowlers went past in their car, and Anna and Bobby waved the little flags they were holding. "We've got to meet some folks," said Mr. Fowler, apologizing for going past.

Louise was thrilled at the long procession of soldiers, and with the loud music of the bands, and the cheering of the crowds, who had come in from all the country around. She stood on the edge of the sidewalk, with Mother and Father, and watched everything with bright, eager eyes. On the tower of the court-house a big flag was floating, high above all

the other flags down below on the buildings
and in the streets. When a flag was carried by
in the procession, the men all took off their
hats. It made Louise feel queer and happy
and excited to see how everybody loved the
flag. She thought of a little poem that Father
had made for Eddie Rickman, on Memorial
Day:

> I take my hat off when the flag
>   Goes by, behind the fife and drum,
> And all the people crowd to see
>   The soldiers, marching as they come.
>
> My father says I must salute
>   The best of all the flags that fly,
> And so I just take off my hat
>   And wave it as the flag goes by.

When the old men from the Soldiers' Home
marched past in their blue uniforms, so different from the khaki of the younger soldiers,
Louise saw tears in Mother's eyes, and she
felt a little lump in her throat, too. There
were not many of the old men left, and they
were all gray and bent, but they tried to hold
themselves straight, and walk with a swing
that kept time to the music. They had "fought

for the Union,'' Mother said, and had stood by Abraham Lincoln in the hard, dark days of the Civil War, when he was working to free the slaves and keep the North and the South together.

"Oh, I hope, I hope that there will never be any more war,'' said Mother. Father had been in the war when Louise was a very little girl, but he never liked to talk about it, and Mother hardly ever said anything about it, either. And now there were big boys marching in the procession, with hoes and rakes and pitch-forks over their shoulders. "Now come the arts of peace,'' said Mother. "I'm so glad.'' Girls were carrying bunches of grain, and milk pails, and baskets of fruit and flowers. Now and then a big decorated wagon (called a float) would pass, and there would be people on it doing peaceful things—piling up sheaves of wheat, or weaving at a loom, or sawing lumber, or planting fruit trees, or sweeping a floor and setting a table. It seemed won-derful to Louise that such things could be shown on a wagon or truck, being driven through the streets.

"I like it almost better than the soldiers," she thought. Now came a group of women who had a flag and a printed sign saying that they were Daughters of the American Revolution. They all wore white dresses and red sashes. "Mother is one of those," said Louise. But Mother lived so far out in the country that she did not get to the meetings or know many of the ladies. Then came boys and girls from the schools, carrying flags and banners. Then there was another band and another group of soldiers marched past, and the procession was over. It had wound around through some of the side streets, and was disbanding at the courthouse yard.

Mrs. Sutherland, the wife of the high school principal, came running up to Mother, and asked all the Martins to go home to dinner with her. She and Mother were from the same college, though they had not been there at the same time, and they had become acquainted last year. "Do come," she said. "I hardly ever see you." And so they went with Mr. and Mrs. Sutherland, and had dinner and stayed a part of the afternoon. There were two large boys in the family, and a baby six months old. The baby had a nurse, a slim, pretty colored girl in a red dress, who laughed a great deal, and let Louise love and cuddle the baby almost as much as she wanted to.

"Yo' dast hold him if you likes," said the nurse.

"Oh, may I?" Louise clapped her hands, and the baby blinked and smiled.

"Jes' sit down solid in that there chair, and I'll put him in yo' arms," said the nurse, showing her white teeth in a grin. So Louise sat down and put out her arms, and took the soft little bundle, and pressed the baby's face against hers, and kissed his tiny hands and dimpled fingers. She held him a long time, and did not want to give him up; but the nurse said, "He's got to have his bottle, now, and go to sleepums." So Louise swung in the hammock, and looked at books, and listened to the grown folks' talk, and then shot off firecrackers with the two big boys in the back yard, until it was time to go home.

It was pleasant to come back to the house on the hill, and to see Flora sitting on the steps. The house was cool, because it had been shut up, and it was full of the scent of flowers, which Little Girl and Mother had put in every room.

"Oh, how nice our house is, Mummy!" cried Louise.

"I think it is, too," answered Mother.

"If it only had a Franklin stove, it would be perfect," said Louise.

"Shsh!" said Mother. But Father was not near enough to hear. "It's too warm now for anything like that, and so we shan't think about it. When the time comes, maybe we'll have one."

"Haven't we had a lovely day?" said Little Girl. "And there's a lot left of it yet. This is our Strawberry Festival, isn't it?" The Martins were to have their first straw-berry shortcake, which was to celebrate the beginning of the strawberry season, as well as the Fourth of July. Mother knew how to make the old-fashioned kind of strawberry shortcake—not the foolish cake-pudding sort that you get in restaurants and hotels (it seems that Father and Mother had both eaten frequently in such places: Louise had hardly seen any). And so they made a game and a gayety out of the first strawberry shortcake of the season.

By the time Mother had changed her frock and looked after the chickens and built up the fire, it was time to get supper. Mother and Louise set out the mahogany table in the sitting room, with the best cross-stitched doilies and centerpiece. In the middle of the table was a loose bunch of purple and white irises and feathery ferns in a clear glass vase. The dishes were the white ones with gold bands, because Mother thought that shortcake didn't "go" with the yellow and orange and green dishes that she used for breakfast and lunch. Louise had polished the silver until it shone "like rivers in the sun," as she said.

The shortcake was to be the main thing, and so there wasn't to be much else. There was cold meat with parsley around it, and a spoonful of creamed potato for each person, and a glass of milk. Mother put the strawberries into a big bowl, and mashed them with plenty of sugar. Then she stirred up a dough like that which she made for baking-powder biscuits. She put this into a shallow tin in two layers, with butter between. While it was baking, the family sat down to the first course. Father had a sweet white rose and bud in his buttonhole, so that he looked very festive, and Mother had a bunch of roses at the waist of her white dotted muslin dress, and you never would have believed that she had worn that same gown for four years.

When they had eaten the first course, Mother went to the kitchen and put the shortcake together, with butter and strawberries and juice. On each plate was a big square, showing richly red against the white china. "I like the looks of it as much as I do the taste," said Mother. She laughed and blushed when Father told her what a good cook she was and how proud he was of her. "And that's what sweetens the strawberries," she said, looking happy.

They sat at the table, talking, while the robins chirruped high in the poplar trees. "Louise and I are the cook's assistants," said

Father, as they got up from the table. "We're going to wash the dishes."

"Oh, yes, we'd like to," said Louise.

"Oh, no," said Mother, "it isn't necessary. There are so few."

"You go and sit down," said Father, "and read that new magazine that you haven't had time to look at."

"It is so tempting," Mother sighed. She took the magazine, and went and sat on the steps. Louise and Father cleared the table in a minute or two, and piled the dishes up in the kitchen.

"I'll wash, Louella-Puella," said Father.

"No, let me," answered Louella. "My sleeves are short."

"Are you sure you can?" asked Father, who was always forgetting how big a girl Louise was growing.

"Of course I can," Louella assured him. "I can stand on this little stool, because the sink is pretty high for me."

So they began washing the dishes, and while they worked, Father sang. He made up a song about the dishes:

"If wishes were fishes,
    We'd go without dishes,
And eat from a leaf or a shell.
We'd go without knives
    The rest of our lives,
And throw all the forks in the well."

"That would leave the spoons," said Louella.

"Spoons are enough for anybody," remarked Father.

"But I don't see what the fishes have to do with it," said Louella, in a puzzled way.

"They *turn the scale* against the dishes," said Father. "Don't you see?"

"No, I don't see." Louella was washing the knives very carefully. "But sing some more, Poppy, won't you?"

"I can't think of any more now," said Father. "I have to think of wiping these dishes dry."

There really were not many dishes, and the two workers had finished almost before they knew it. "Everything is as clean as a whistle," said Louella, as she hung up her dishcloth.

Mother came in, with the magazine in her hand. "I heard you people shouting and laughing," she said. "I thought perhaps you were having more fun than I was."

"We love to wash dishes," said Little Girl.

"I'll let you do it all the time, then," laughed Mother.

"It might not be so much fun. But we always have good times when we're together, don't we, Father?" Louella slipped her hand into his.

"We surely do, my Pet," was the reply. "Now, it will soon be time for the fireworks."

As the dusk was falling, the Martins walked down to Mr. Rickman's, where the fireworks were to be displayed. A good many people in town had given money to buy them, and nearly all the little village was there to see the beautiful bright "flowers in the sky," as Louise called them.

Mr. Rickman and Father set them off. First came the pinwheels, and some of the Roman candles, with their brilliant fountains of colored lights. Then the skyrockets roared and flashed their way into the dark, and slowly plunged down with a trail of stars and sparks in their wake. "Don't you love it, dear?" said Mother.

"It's lovely, lovely," whispered Little Girl. "I can't tell you how I like it. Oh, there's another, and it's the brightest yet. Oo-oo, what a roar it makes!"

It was late before the last flower of light had faded, and the thick darkness settled down upon the group of village people. Louella-Puella, tired and sleepy, walked home with her arm around Mother's waist. "It seems a long time since morning," she said, "but it's been one of the nicest days I can remember. All summer I can go on thinking about the Fourth of July."

CHAPTER VII

STRAWBERRIES

The next day there were six quarts of berries to sell to Mr. Rickman, and the day after that, the picking began in earnest. It was better to pick the berries in the afternoon, when the dew had dried, and this was the warmest part of the day; so the work was hard. Father picked long and fast, but the berries ripened faster than he could gather them, and he hired Jerome Kingsley to help him. Jerome was a boy who lived in the village and went to the high school in the larger town. He was having a vacation now, and he was earning money to buy his clothes and books when he went back to school in the fall. He had black hair and brown eyes and red cheeks, and he was tall, with straight, thin shoulders. "Jerome's a good worker," Father said, "because he knows what he's working for, and what it's all about."

So Father and Jerome picked berries all the afternoon, and sometimes Mother and Louella went out and helped for an hour or so, though Father would never let them work very long. "We'll pick at least what we use in the house," said Mother, "and maybe a few more."

Father took Louella with him when he made his first trip to deliver his berries at the hotel on the Upper Lakes. He piled the crates of berries into the car, on the floor and on the back seat. "Come on, Pigeon," he said, and "flew" Louella into the front seat. Then he jumped in, himself. Away they went, down the hill and around through the village, Louella holding her hat. They passed Mr. Anson's big house with the cupola, and two or three smaller houses, and went up the hill, which Ann Eliza took gallantly. The next that they saw was the McFadden Farm, with its long red sheds and huge red and white barns, its towering silos and windmills, and its small, old-fashioned white house.

"It looks like a white sheep among a lot of big red cows, doesn't it?" said Louella.

"It does that," said Father, laughing.

There were other farms and pastures and woodlands, and then there was a turn in the road, near the Soldiers' Home, that took it in among overhanging trees, and brought it out behind the Island View Hotel. "How do you like coming to the back door, Louise?" asked Father.

"I don't care," answered Louella, looking up at him affectionately.

"I don't either," said Father.

It was really a side door, and a handsome man without a coat came out and said, "How do you do?" to Father. They shook hands. "How are things going?" the man inquired.

"Finely," said Father. "How does the hotel start in?"

"Splendidly. The warm weather has helped us." The man turned toward Louella. "Is this your little girl? Shucks! How she has grown."

"Yes, she's a big girl," said Father. He lifted the cover from one of the crates.

"Say, those are top-notchers, aren't they?" said the man.

"Pretty good," said Father; "but we'll have better. The first ones aren't always the best."

"These are great."

A colored porter came and carried the crates of berries into the building.

"You'll get your check at the office," said the man whom they had been talking with. "Now, I know what this little girl would like. Ice cream. Am I right, eh?"

"She usually does," smiled Father. Louella only got red and squirmed. The man went into the house, and came back with a big dish of ice cream. It was pink and white, with nuts sprinkled on top.

"Thank you," said Louella, finding her tongue.

While she was eating the ice cream, Father and the other man were talking about the hotel. "I want to show you the new ice house," said the steward, and he and Father walked away. The ice cream was good, and Louella made it last quite a long time. The colored man grinned at her, and said, "Pretty grand, ain't it?" Louise did not know what to say to him, so she merely nodded and said nothing.

She stared at the grounds out in front of the hotel, where little girls like herself were running around in white dresses and white shoes and stockings. Louella thought that nothing would make her happier than to run and play with them.

Father came back, and took her with him into the office. Ladies in light, thin dresses were passing back and forth on the veranda and in the halls, and men in white flannel trousers and gray or white coats were walking here and there. "Don't they have anything to do but just have a good time?" asked Louella, as she and Father went out at the side door of the office.

"It seems not," said Father absently. They walked out to the top of the hill and looked out across the lake, where rowboats and canoes were crawling about, and little launches were puffing and sailboats gliding over the water. Boys in bathing were splashing and shouting. Flags and pennants were flying at the dock.

Oh, how Louella wanted to stay and look around, and run down the hill to the lake, and ride in a launch, and go in bathing!

"I'll have to bring you over some day, and see that you get a ride," said Father.

Louella squeezed his hand. That was what she wanted, so much that she could hardly keep from jumping up and down. "Can't to-day," he went on. "We aren't dressed for it, and the berries are waiting to be picked, and Mother expects us back." Louella nodded and winked back the tears, so that Father shouldn't see them. It seemed as if she couldn't go. They walked slowly back to the car and got in, and they went home a different way— around by the Indian Crossing. They stopped at Anna's house for a minute, but they could not stay, for Father was in a hurry to get home. Louise kept thinking about the happy little girls in the white dresses, and the gasoline launches puffing up and down the lake, and she did not have much to say. When they got home, Mother looked tired, and Jerome was drinking ginger water because he was so warm. Some campers came up in their car and wanted to buy ten quarts of berries, and there was a crate to be taken to Mr. Rickman's store.

The afternoon was dull, except for the snake. Louella was walking up the path, late in the afternoon, when she saw something wriggling in the grass. "Oo-oo!" she screamed. "Oo-oo! Maybe it's a snake." And she ran toward the house. Father came toward her, not very hastily. "Oh, look! it's in the sand. It's a real snake. See, Father!"

"Yes, I see," said Father. "What about it?"

"But it's a snake!" The children at school had made Louella think that she ought to be afraid of snakes.

"Well, my child, it's nothing but a harmless little garter snake," said Father. "Come here and see how handsome he is."

"N-no," said Louella, backing farther away. "I don't think I want to."

"Come on." Father held out his hand, and drew her close to him. They leaned over and saw the gleaming colors on the scales of the snake, and the fine creamy skin on its under side. "I want you to get a better look at him," said Father.

"This is near enough." Louella shrank away.

Father put out his hand and grasped the snake quickly, just below the neck. It twisted and turned about, its bright scales shining in the sun. "Now take a look," said Father. Louella examined its smooth, flat head, with the bright black eyes and tiny red mouth. "Put your hand on it," Father urged her. "Feel its scales."

Louella put out her hand timidly, but drew it back again, as the snake gave a jump in Father's hand. "Won't it really hurt?" she asked.

"It couldn't hurt you if it tried," answered Father.

Louella put her hand on the glossy scales. "It's awfully pretty," she said. "I didn't think it looked as nice as that."

Father let it go, and it wriggled away for a distance, and hid under the overhanging bushes. "See how graceful he is," said Father. "His going is as easy as thinking. And now," he went on, "you won't ever be afraid of a common garter snake again, will you?"

"No, I should say not," Louella replied. "But you know, Father, the boys and girls all run and scream, 'Kill the snake, kill the snake!' and they throw stones at it, too."

"That's foolish and cruel," said Father. "It wants to live, and it doesn't do any harm in the world. I suppose it does some good, eating up insects. Let's see. Can't I write something about it?" He took paper and pencil from his pocket, and scribbled for a few minutes. "There's a rhyme for you, missy," he said at last. And then he read his verses aloud:

The Garter Snake

"One day a snake came through our yard;
  I saw it wriggling in the sand,
And Father ran and picked it up,
  And held it in his hand.

Its back was all a bluish green,
  That shone like jewels in the light,
With yellow bands; and underneath
  Its skin was creamy white.

It twisted round and in and out,
And curled up in a gleaming ring:
I never thought a snake could be
So beautiful a thing!"

"Thank you, Poppy," said Little Girl. "I'm going to try to do this on the typewriter."

"Better let me help you," answered Father. "Just now I have to go on with the strawberries." But later Louella did write the poem out, with one finger, on the typewriter, and she did not make so very many mistakes.

A day or two after this something happened which brought about a day of happiness. Little Girl was in the kitchen feeding Flora an extra saucer of milk, and she heard some one come to the sitting-room door, and then she heard her Mother say, "Why, how do you do, Mrs. Fellows? And Mr. Fellows—and Harry?" Louise remembered the people whom she liked so much who had come last year to buy raspberries and blackberries. "This is a surprise," Mother was saying, "we didn't know that you were back."

"We're here earlier than we were last year," said Mrs. Fellows.

"We couldn't wait to get back," said Mr. Fellows in his deep voice. "Harry could hardly wait. Where's your little Louise?"

"She's right here," answered Mother. "Come in, Louise, and see Mr. and Mrs. Fellows and Harry." Louise came in shyly. "You remember them, don't you, dear?"

"Oh, yes!" Louise replied. She shook hands with them all. Father would not have her taught to curtsey, for he thought that sort of thing rather foolish. Harry was as awkward as Louise, who was about his age, and fumbled at her hand and then let go of it, in a clumsy way. He was a thin-faced, tanned, sober boy, with light brown hair, almost the color of his face. His blue eyes were bright and friendly.

Mother and the other grown-up people were talking about the cottages at the lakes, and about the berry crop and such matters. Louise could not think of anything to say to Harry except, "Are you going to stay here all summer?"

"I guess so," said Harry. "I hope so.

Oh, say! We've got a tame squirrel at our cottage!"

"Oh, *have* you?" answered Little Girl, quite excited.

"Yes, sir," Harry went on. "The first day we were there, he came right down on the porch, and now he eats out of our hands, and he runs in and out, just like a dog."

"Isn't that queer?" said Louise.

"He must be one of those that we coaxed around the house last summer," said Harry. "He seemed awful glad to have us back."

"We've got a squirrel up in the back lot," said Louise, eager to tell her story, too; "but he keeps away from the house. I guess he's afraid of Flora."

"Yes, I remember your cat," answered Harry, "but I couldn't think what her name was."

"Louise must come up and see us," Mrs. Fellows said, putting her hand on Little Girl's shoulder. "May she come soon, Mrs. Martin? The launches are running now. Why not let her come up and have a ride with us on the lakes?"

"Oh!" Louise jumped up and clapped her hands. What Mrs. Fellows had suggested was exactly what she wanted to do.

"Do you want to go, Louise?" asked Mother.

"Oh, *do* I? Of course I want to just awfully, Mother," answered Little Girl.

"We'll take very good care of her," said Mr. Fellows.

"We-ell," began Mother. She did not like to have Little Girl go away without her. "I think we can spare her for a little while. We'll see what her father says."

Louise ran out to where Father was putting boxes of berries into a crate. "Oh, Poppy," she cried, "the Fellowses are here—you know, they were here last year—and they want me to go up and visit them, and they'll take me on the lakes!"

"M-m-m," said Father, marking down something on a paper.

"May I go, Poppy? Mother will let me if you will."

"Why, I suppose so," said Father. He didn't like to have Little Girl go away with other people, either.

"Is it *yes?*"

"Yes, it's *yes.*" Father smiled at the eager face of his daughter.

Louise flew back, and said to Mrs. Fellows, "Father says *yes,* so it's *yes!*"

"Good!" said Mr. Fellows, who was a tall, heavy man, with a kind, smiling face. Harry only grinned, after the manner of boys.

"Can you let us have five quarts of strawberries?" Mrs. Fellows was saying to Mother. In the midst of the talk, it was arranged that Louise should go the next day to visit the Fellows family, and that they should come after her.

Mr. Fellows and Harry came, in the forenoon, in a pretty little car, much nicer than Ann Eliza, as even Little Girl could see. "How nice you look," said Mr. Fellows, noticing Louise's fresh blue chambray frock and the white hat with the daisies. Mr. Fellows was a "noticing" sort of man, who did not think that he was too old to be interested in children. "We'll take the best sort of care of her, Mrs. Martin."

Mother kissed Louise, and then waved at her

from the gate. It did not take the little car very long to whirl along the road to the place where it must turn to go to the lakes. It had to go slowly through the marsh and up the low hill and among the thick-standing tree trunks. There was a beautiful coolness and quiet in the woods, where the only sounds were the twittering of birds and the chattering of hidden squirrels.

All at once the car spurted into an open space, and there was the cottage, painted white, with wide, screened porches.

Mrs. Fellows came running out. "Well, here we are!" she cried. She helped Louise out of the car, and held her hand. "I want you to feel that you're right at home," she said.

"Whoo-hoo!" Harry had scrambled out of the car, and was looking here and there. "I want you to see Squirr'ly-Wirr'ly," he was saying. "There he is! There he is! Don't talk loud." (He had been shouting himself.) "Are there some nuts, Mummy? Wait!" He ran in and got a handful of peanuts, and gave half of them to Louise.

The squirrel came scampering near, with his handsome furry tail held high upon his back. He stopped and sat up, and Harry threw him a nut. The squirrel took it in his tiny black and gray hands, tore it apart with his teeth, and ate the white kernel hurriedly, as if he were afraid of not getting any more.

"Oh, the dear little thing," said Louise, with a squeal of pleasure.

"Here, now, you coax him up to you," said Harry.

Louise crouched down and held out a nut. "Come, petty," she called, "come and take it." The squirrel cocked his head to look at her with his sharp, knowing eyes, and then came creeping forward. Louise gasped when he put up his paws and took hold of her fingers. He snatched the nut from her, and then got down to eat it, nibbling rapidly at the shell and throwing it away. "Isn't he the nicest little fellow?" she whispered. It seemed as if she couldn't tell any one how much she loved the beautiful little creature.

"Have him get on your knee," whispered Harry.

Louise held the next nut higher, and Mr. Squirrel took hold of her dress and pulled himself up to her knee with his clinging claws, and then sat there to eat the nut she gave him. She could hardly keep from laughing aloud, because his feet tickled her knee, and he looked so comical with the peanut in his hands, and his pretty little face so serious over his feast. She moved, and he jumped down and ran a few feet away. "Oh, I love him," she said. "He's a little pet thing."

"Isn't it wonderful to have him so tame?" said Harry. He was proud of the small, friendly animal, whose love he had won with kindness.

After Squirr'ly-Wirr'ly had had his fill and run away to the treetops, there were other things to do. There was the house to see, and Harry's room, where he had a flag, and a school pennant, and a wasp's nest (with no wasps in it), and a baseball mask and mitt, and a good many other interesting articles, such as shells and bunches of moss, and bright-colored pebbles, and even some Indian arrowheads. On the wall were pictures from the covers of magazines, and on the cot-bed there was a bright red blanket, so that the bed became a couch. On the table was a pile of books. Louise could hardly keep her hands off them, but she knew that it would not be polite to sit down and read when she was visiting; so she tried to keep her eyes turned away from the books.

"I've got a book on natural history," said Harry. He ran through the pages, flipping them with his thumb, and Louise caught glimpses of marvelous beasts and birds. Harry must have understood how she longed to look at them, for he said, "Wouldn't you like to take this home with you, when you go? We can get it back any time."

"Oh, I'd just love it." Louise felt grateful to Harry for understanding how much she wanted the book.

"See, I've got a magnifying glass," said Harry, eager to show off his treasures. It was a round glass with a handle.

"Oh, let me see." Little Girl took the glass in her fingers, and held it over a piece of moss. The feathery green sprays and tiny red cups grew taller before her eyes, and stood out like a fairy forest. The glass was a delightful thing to have. She held it over everything on the table—flowers, a printed card, a kodak picture of the Fellows family on their porch at home. "Oo-o! I can see it all so *plain*," she cried. She could hardly bear to put the glass down.

"Show Louise your Mah Jong set," said Mrs. Fellows from the doorway.

Louise lifted the colored tiles one by one and looked at them, pleased and puzzled. "Can you play?" asked Harry. Louise shook her head. "Well, we'll show you how," the boy went on. Could she learn such a queer game? Louise was saying to herself.

They went out on the screened porch where there was a hammock and a couch with cushions. The lake lay below them, smooth and shining. A white rowboat with scarlet trimmings was tied at the dock. Louise could hear sounds as of setting a table. "Just time to run down to the dock before lunch and get a good look at the lake," said Mrs. Fellows.

Louise and Harry ran down the hill, and

clattered out upon the dock. Honeysuckle
vines and June-berry bushes hung over the
water. The big round June-berries were almost ripe. Louise could look far down the
lake in one direction and see a farmhouse with
big red barns; but not so far in the other
direction, because the lake took a turn beyond
a tamarack swamp. "That's the mouth of
the creek over there," said Harry. "It's great
to go up the creek. You have to pole the
boat most of the time."

"Har-ree!" called Mrs. Fellows. "Lunch
is ready."

"We're coming!" shouted Harry.

The two children ran up the hill and into
the dining room at the side of the cottage.
There were many good things for luncheon,
including huckleberry pie. Louise was shy,
and did not talk much. She was afraid that
her mouth was blue from the pie, but she ate
every crumb, because it was so good. There
was a maid who brought the dishes in and
took them away.

After the meal was over, they all sat out
on the porch for a few minutes, looking at

some picture papers. Then three short *toots* sounded from down the lake. "It's the launch, the launch, the launch," chanted Harry. "It's coming to take us on."

Mrs. Fellows put on her hat and silk gloves, and took her Japanese umbrella; Mr. Fellows put on his thin summer coat. Harry was ready without doing anything, except that his mother sent him to wash his hands.

"You don't need to wear your hat unless you want to," she said to Louise, and Little Girl was glad to leave her hat.

Now the boat came nearer, with long, warning *toots*. Louise and her friends ran down the hill, and were on the dock when the boat came rushing up, chugging through the water with swift, smooth motions. How exciting it was to step in over the cushioned seats and sit down under the awning!

"*Toot-toot!*" called Harry. The whistle shrieked, the boat churned and shivered as it backed out from the pier and turned toward the end of the lake. Then it darted forward again like a big fish cutting the water.

Louise sat close to Mrs. Fellows, though she

was not exactly timid. She felt the spray like a fine mist as the wind dashed it against her face.

The boat went to the far end of the lake, close to the farmhouse, where two children, a boy and a girl, were playing in a meadow full of tall grass and irises. They ran down to a long plank pier, and waved to the people on the boat. Louise knew how they felt. She knew that they would like to go along. But soon the boat had scudded on, and left the two children a long way behind. Louise turned and waved once more, because she felt sorry for them. Now the boat was flying along the shore, where there was a cottage with people sitting on the porch, and a long-legged dog standing on the dock and barking with all his might. Then they passed the Fellows cottage, high on the bank among the trees.

"I suppose Squirr'ly-Wirr'ly is up on a branch looking at us," said Harry.

On and on they went, the spray blowing and the wind lifting Louise's curls. Mr. Fellows held on to his hat and then took it off. They went through a deep lake where the water was so blue that it was almost black, and then through a shallow one, where the sand showed at the bottom, and the bulrushes grew thick along the shoals. They passed launches and rowboats full of fishermen or pleasure seekers. The boat entered a narrow creek called the Indian Crossing and puffed slowly along, while echoes could be heard from the wall of trees on each side. The echoes grew loud and hollow under the wooden bridge.

"Wouldn't I like to see the Indians that used to cross the river here!" said Harry.

"I can imagine that I see them," said Mrs. Fellows: "Ponies and dogs and squaws and papooses, and the big tall warriors stalking along by themselves, with their bows and arrows—it would be a great sight."

"Hundreds of arrowheads have been found around here," said Mr. Fellows.

"Oh, I wish I could hunt for some," cried Harry. But the boat was hurrying now, to make up for lost time. There were neatly painted cottages to be seen, with flags flying in front of them on tall poles. Children were

playing and bathing on the shore. Pretty
little sailboats skimmed across the water, with
their sails shining in the sun. More cottages
and more people appeared, more boats and
bathers.

"We're getting near the hotel," said Mrs.
Fellows; and before long they were drawing
up at a pier with a small shop built at the
side of it.

"Island View Hotel," called the skipper.

"Time for ice cream," laughed Mr. Fellows.

It was the same place that Louise had seen
when she and Father had come to the hotel
with strawberries; but now she was looking
up instead of looking down from the top of
the bank. They all got out of the launch and
went into the shop, where there were two
tables with marble tops. They sat down and
had ice cream with maple sirup and nuts on it,
the best that Louise had ever eaten, she
thought.

"Isn't it *good?*" said Mrs. Fellows.

"It's the cat's whiskers," said Harry, feeling proud to say what he had heard from the

older boys. Louise hardly knew what he meant. She bought a little box of candy for her mother.

"Let's go up the hill," said Mr. Fellows. "The band's playing." They went up the hill. So there was Louise in her pretty dress, walking around with the ladies and gentlemen, just as she had seen other girls doing when she and Father had been there. The music was gay, and the people were gay, too, laughing and calling to one another, and planning what they were going to do during the afternoon. It was as exciting as a game to watch them. Mr. Fellows went away for a minute, and came back with some tickets. "There's a moving picture that starts at two o'clock," he said. "Do you youngsters want to see it? It's Jackie Coogan——"

"Oo-oo, I want to, I want to," cried Louise, forgetting everything but the pictures.

"I want to, I want to!" said Harry, so loudly that everybody turned to look.

"Will you take the kids?" said Mr. Fellows to his wife. "I'd rather stay outside, if you don't mind."

"Of course I'll take them," said Mrs. Fellows, reaching for the tickets. "I'd love to see Jackie myself."

Louise could hardly believe that she was going to the moving pictures. She hadn't counted on that. She kept hold of Mrs. Fellows' hand, as they went into the darkened room. Then there followed two hours of happiness and excitement, watching the adventures of the boy actor. Louise had actually never seen Jackie Coogan before, and she could not help thinking how splendid it would be to tell Mother and Father about him. But she forgot where she was, almost, and all that was going on outside, while she gazed breathlessly at the scenes upon the curtain.

When they came out, blinking and chattering, it seemed to Louise that there was nothing more that she wanted. But now Mr. Fellows had another surprise. "It's time to go in bathing," he said as he met them outside the door; "the youngsters will have to have a dip before we go."

"I like our own lake, but it's more fun here," said Harry. So Mr. Fellows hired bathing suits for Louise and Harry, and they went in with all the other boys and girls along the shore from the hotel and the cottages, while Mr. and Mrs. Fellows sat on the bank and watched them. It was fun to splash and plunge with the others, and watch them dive from the raft and jump from the springboard. There were two big men from the hotel, in bathing suits, watching all the time to see that the children were safe.

The "dip" was over all too soon. When the two children were dressed, Mr. Fellows went to engage a launch to take them all home. Presently they had climbed into the launch again—it seemed a long time since they had come—and then they were off for a trip through the last two lakes of the chain, where the islands were and the sulphur springs, and more cottages and boarding houses. This was the prettiest part of all. Louise squeezed Mrs. Fellows' hand and said, "Oh, I'm so glad you brought me."

"I'm glad, too," answered Mrs. Fellows, squeezing Little Girl's hand.

The trip back was like another flight with

wings, with the rush of the boat through the water, and the wind and the spray in the faces of the passengers. It was getting toward supper time when they arrived at the dock in front of the Fellows' cottage. Mrs. Fellows made Louise lie down in the hammock for a rest, and Harry had to lie down on the couch. But Harry sat up, saying, "You know, we were going to play Mah Jong, and we haven't played a bit, and you haven't seen my tent, down on the Point, and we haven't been after bird cherries."

"Oh, dear," sighed Little Girl from her cushions, "there's such a lot to do, that a day is hardly long enough."

"You'll have to come again before long," said Mrs. Fellows from the doorway. "Perhaps you can play Mah Jong a very little after supper, for it doesn't get dark early."

"Mother'll be expecting me," said Louise. There was time after supper for a half hour with the Mah Jong tiles, and then Louise put them down, and said, "Please, I think I'd better go home."

Mr. Fellows got out the car, and Harry ran

to get the natural history book, and the whole family took Louise home.

Louise threw her arms around her mother's neck. "Oh, I've had such a lovely, lovely day," she said. And then she whispered, "But I'm so glad to get home." Flora was rubbing around her ankles and purring, and Father was singing a funny song that Louise liked, about Noah and the Ark, beginning:

"Noah of old he built de ark—
  Sing polly-wolly-doodle all de day—
He built it out of hickory bark—
  Sing polly-wolly-doodle all de day."

Mother was washing the dishes, and Louise wiped them just as if she had been there all day. And then she sat down on the back steps to cuddle Flora. The stars came out and the tree toads were squeaking in some mysterious nook. "I'm so sleepy," yawned Little Girl, "but, Mother, I really must have a magnifying glass."

CHAPTER VIII

A TREASURE FROM THE ATTIC

Now the days were going on, faster and faster, every one of them full of work and play from morning to night. Louise did not go away from home very much, except when Father took her and Mother out for a ride in the coolness of the evening. Father was busy all day long; in the morning with his writing (now that he had finished his book, he was doing shorter things) and in the afternoon and evening with his garden and his berries and the chickens, and ever so many tasks that had to be attended to.

"Poor Father is working pretty hard," said Mother. "I wish we could make it easier for him. We must be as nice to him as we can."

He did not hear from the book, but almost every day a long envelope would come with some of Father's writings in it that somebody didn't want. Once in a while, there would be a thinner envelope, and in it there would be a blue slip of paper that was a check, and then Father and Mother would smile, and Mother would call Father "our genius," and Father would try to look as if he didn't like it, when he really did. But it seemed that the checks were never for very large sums of money, and they always had to go for something the family needed, such as a new tire for Ann Eliza, or a sprayer for the apple trees, or new shingles for the house, or wood for the stoves, or something of that kind; and, of course, all the time there had to be money to pay Mr. Rickman for the groceries, and the oil man for oil and gasoline, and other people for other things. Louise did not hear much about these matters, but once in a while she heard her father and mother talking, and she knew that the year before (especially the winter) had been hard for them, and that they were hoping for easier times.

Louise helped with the housework and with

the chickens, but most of the time she was free to enjoy herself. Other children came to the house—Anna and Bobby Fowler, and Eddie Rickman, and Amy Colter, and Ella Kingsley (Jerome's sister), and Harry Fellows who liked to have a good romp wtih a crowd of children, in spite of all his pleasure at the cottage.

One afternoon the children went for wintergreens, trooping first through the orchard, where the hard, green little apples were hanging on the trees. Eddie picked one and bit into it. He spat it out in a hurry, and his face was twisted with the sourness of it. They all laughed at his funny expression. Then they hunted for wild strawberries in the grass —the small wild berries which are so much scarcer and sweeter than the big garden berries. "Here's one," "Here's another," they called, and every one had smeary fingers from the red juice. Here and there the wild raspberries were getting ripe, and branches of red bird cherries, delightfully sour, hung down within reach of the children's arms.

"I'd like to be a bird, and live on bird cherries," said Eddie.

"What would you do when they were gone?" asked practical Anna.

"Oh, there'd be something else," said Eddie.

Now they were in among the trees of the woods, where the grass was thin, and red and yellow and orange mushrooms had pushed their way up through the black soil. It was quiet in the woods, except for the chirping of birds and the caw of a lonely crow.

"Oh, wintergreens!" the children all shouted at once, and fell to gathering the slender sprays of rounded leaves, young and tender and spicy. Every one was chewing them, and picking handfuls to take home. Wintergreen berries were scarce, but a few still clung to the older stems. Louise put all she found into her pocket, to take home to Mother, who liked them especially well.

Louise remembered a poem that Father had made for her last year, about wintergreens. She mumbled it to herself as she picked and ate:

Wintergreens

"Just over the hill, in a wood that I know,
There's a dim, dusky hollow where winter-
greens grow.
The leaves are all fragrant and shining and
round,
With slender brown stems clinging close to
the ground.
The berries are crimson and spicy and
sweet:
They look like red apples for fairies to eat."

"What are you muttering about?" asked
Anna.

"Nothing much," said Little Girl.

They romped about in the woods, playing
tag and dodging among the trees, calling and
shouting as loudly as they wished. Eddie
Rickman stood up and *who-hoo-ed* and whistled
through his fingers.

"What you doing that for?" asked Harry.

"It's such fun to yell as loud as I want to,"
said Eddie, "without any one saying, 'Oh,
what a terrible noise!'"

"I like that, too," said Harry. *"Whoo-
hoo! Whoo-hoo!"*

"Oh, dear, what an awful noise," said Amy Colter.

Everybody laughed. "It's no use," said Eddie, grinning. "Even out here there's somebody that wants us to stop."

"I guess you've made noise enough, anyhow," said Anna. "Let's play hide and coop, going home."

At the edge of the woods, they "counted out" to see who should blind. The lot fell to Eddie, and he put his arm up against a tree, and put his eyes against his arm, and began counting up to a hundred. The other children scattered, sinking quickly out of sight.

Louise scampered away, and hid behind a big gray rock. This did not seem secure enough. She could hear Eddie counting— "fifty-six, fifty-seven, fifty-eight." She ran as hard as she could to the field of grain, where Mr. Calkins' land came next to Father's. There was a low stone wall with an old rail fence at the top. Over she went, all out of breath, and sat down among the tall rye stalks. They were yellow as gold, and almost ripe enough to cut. The long tassels at the ends dipped and swayed in the wind. Louise forgot to call out "Coo-oop" to show that she was hidden. She thought, "I'm like a little rabbit scrooching down in here." She laughed to herself. "I'll be as still as a rabbit, too; but I can't make my nose go up and down in such a funny way." She sat trying to wrinkle her nose as a bunny does, but she gave it up, and cuddled down as still as any little creature of the fields. The loveliness of the place came over her. She was only a little girl, but, better than some grown-up people could, she felt the beauty that lay in the blueness of the sky, with the few white clouds floating far up, and the close, yellow brightness of the grain, with its soft, dipping motion and noiseless swaying. The dark green of the trees was just showing beyond the fence, and wild morning-glory vines were climbing along the rails. In the grass close to the fence, there were delicate sprays of fringed purple flowers, and coarser yellow and white ones. A bluebird sailed low, just skimming the top of the grain; then a swallow darted and soared over the field as if he were dizzy with joy and could not keep from dancing. Little Girl, watching him, fell into a kind of dream, feeling a strange, warm happiness as she snuggled into her nest among the tall stalks of grain. "The beautifulness of it," she kept saying to herself.

She sat there so long that the other children had all been found, and they were calling and wondering where she was. After a while, she saw Anna's head come up over the wall, and then Anna gave a loud call to the others, "Whoo-hoo! Here she is!" she cried. And then she said to Louise, "We've hunted and hunted for you, and you never said a word. I don't believe you even called *coop* when you were hid."

Louise got up, looking guilty, and shook the sand out of her skirts. "I—I'm afraid I didn't. I forgot."

"Forgot!" said Anna wonderingly. "Why, how could you *forget?* Weren't you playing?"

"Yes—but—I was thinking about something else." Louise always found it hard to explain herself to Anna.

"I think it's awfully queer," said Anna.

The others came running up, saying, ''You're caught, you're caught,'' and Louise climbed over the fence and went home with them. She did not say much, but she kept thinking about the wonderful blue of the sky and the yellow of the grain field, and the joyous free sweep of the swallows as they darted above her head.

On the way home, they saw a little field mouse creeping through the grass, a small, brown, frightened thing, glad to hide away in a tuft of grass from the tramping feet of the children. And they saw a squirrel, too, on the branch of a tree. He was scolding and chittering as if he were vexed at being interrupted in his work of storing seeds and grain. He was not so tame as Harry's squirrel.

At home that evening, Louise told her father about the mouse and the squirrel, and he made up two poems for her and wrote them out on the typewriter.

THE SQUIRREL

Oh, little Mr. Squirrel Fur,
A-sitting in your tree,
Now why are you so very cross,
And scolding so at me?

You shake your saucy little head,
And flirt your tail of gray:
Do you believe I want to take
The nuts you've stowed away?

Now, silly Mr. Squirrel-Fur,
You needn't be afraid;
I've all the nuts I want at home,
And cake and lemonade.

But even if I wanted nuts,
And they were very few,
I'm sure I never should forget
To leave enough for you.

So, little Mr. Squirrel-Fur,
You mustn't scold at me;
You've nothing to be cross about,
A-sitting in your tree!

THE FIELD MOUSE

Little mouse, pretty mouse,
In your coat of brown,
Do you think you like the fields
Better than the town?
When you make that funny squeak,
What is it you say?
Little mouse, pretty mouse,
Do not run away!

Little mouse, pretty mouse,
Are you all alone?
Do you have a furry nest
Underneath a stone?
Are there baby mousies there,
Pink and soft and wee?
Little mouse, pretty mouse,
I should like to see!

There were many days when Louise and
Anna enjoyed their playhouse in the orchard,
and, when it rained, Louise always thought of
the playhouse out in the downpour. Father
had made a wooden cover for the stove, as
he had said he would do. Also, he had made
a seat or bench out of a board nailed to two
other boards, which was much nicer than the
"sofa" which the girls had made for themselves. Anna's father had made a cupboard
by putting shelves in a shallow wooden box,
which could stand up solidly against a tree.
Anna's mother had found an old table which
she could spare, and Mr. Martin had sawed
off the legs a bit, so that it would be the
right height for the girls. Mr. Rickman at
the store had given them some tea matting
for rugs. To the ten-cent-store dishes they

had added some basins and two cooking spoons and a sharp knife, and they had two dish towels made from flour sacks, and a tablecloth made from a piece of an old sheet. They were rather proud of their playhouse, and spent all the time they could in it—that is, when there were not many other things to do.

Anna loved to cook, and sometimes it was hard for Louise to be as much interested as Anna was.

"I know what I'm going to do," said Anna one day. "I'm going to make some jam."

"Jam!" said Louise. "Isn't that awfully hard? What kind are you going to make?"

"Rawsberry," answered Anna promptly.

"Father calls it ras'berry," said Louise before she thought.

"*I* call it rawsberry," Anna replied. "Anyway, I don't care what it's called. I'm going to make some."

"All right," said Louise. She wanted to be polite, but she could not get very much excited over jam.

"We'll pick the berries up in the lot next

to the woods," said Anna. "There's sugar in the jar that Mother gave us."

So the girls went and picked the ripe red raspberries in the hot sun. They had about a quart when they had finished. Then the fire had to be built and coaxed along until it was hot. "Isn't it lovely to see the smoke coming out of the chimney!" sighed Anna, clasping her hands. That chimney gave her more pleasure than anything else that could be imagined.

"Are you sure you can do it?" asked Mrs. Martin, when the girls ran to ask her how the jam was to be made. "It takes quite a long time, you know."

"We have plenty of time," said Anna.

Mother smiled. "I suppose you have." Then she went on, "Well, cook your berries in just a tiny bit of water, because they're so juicy themselves; and then measure exactly what you have, and put in exactly as much sugar, and boil it till it gets thick."

"That's easy," commented Anna. "We can do that."

The basin sat up proudly on the tin top of the stove, as if it knew how important a part it had to play in making the jam. It held the fresh raspberries and "a tiny bit" of water; and pretty soon the boiling began.

"How nice it smells!" said Anna, wiping a spoon very clean, to stir the berries with. They certainly did have a delicious smell, Louise thought.

The measuring was the best part, when the berries had "boiled up." There were five little tin cupfuls of the hot berries and juice. The sugar had to be measured, so that there were five cupfuls, too. It was thrilling to put the mixture back on the stove, and see the red juice creeping up into the white sugar. Louise had to put more wood into the stove, because Anna hung over the boiling berries and could not be dragged away.

A long time they crouched over the stove in the warm afternoon sun. The wind cooled their hot faces, and rattled the leaves and green apples on the trees around them. Flora lay in the grass, with her paw curled over her eyes, to keep out the light while she slept.

"Mother has her jelly glasses in hot water when she fills them," said Anna. "But where are our glasses?"

They hadn't thought about disposing of the jam when it was made. Louise ran to the house, and of course Mother had exactly what was needed—a flock of small glasses just right for a playhouse table. Anna was stirring and stirring and tasting, and nearly all the playhouse dishes were smeared with the crimson jam.

"Let me stir," begged Louise, eager for her share of the thrills. But in a few minutes the spoon was back in Anna's hand.

"It's thick, it's jelling," cried Anna anxiously. "Won't you ask your Mother if she'll come and look at it? Do you s'pose she would?"

Louise sped through the tall grass to the kitchen door. "Oh, Mummy, will you come and look at the jam?" she called.

Mother came hurrying, for too much cooking might spoil the precious jam, and that would be a pity. She lifted the spoon and let the thick red juice drip down, and then she cooled some on a broken plate. "It's just right, I do believe," she said, almost as interested as Anna. "Are your glasses all ready? In hot water? Good! Anna, you dip out the jam into the glasses."

Flora woke up and yawned and looked on. It was a breathless moment when Anna dipped out a spoonful and dripped it into the first little glass. She filled that one, and went on to the next.

"Oo-oo, let me!" Louise dipped out the jam and filled two glasses. Anna finished the number.

In a few minutes there was a row of the full glasses on the table. Anna, with her cheeks red and her eyes shining and her hair tousled, stood back and looked and looked at them. "Aren't they lovely?" she kept saying. "Aren't they the loveliest things?" The sun shone through the clear glass and the red fruit and juice.

"I know how you feel, Anna," said Mother. "I always feel like that when I've made a lot of jam or jelly."

"It's the most fun," said Anna, scraping the basin and eating the morsels on her spoon. "Oh, I just wish I could cook all the time."

"I guess you're going to be a cook when you grow up," said Louise.

"I guess I am," answered Anna happily.

After the dishes were washed and put away, Eddie and Amy arrived, and they all played *pum-pum-pull-away* between the fence and the schoolhouse, till they were tired out.

That evening, as Louise sat on the steps, reading a book which Harry Fellows had lent her (she had been up at his cottage again, and had played Mah Jong and gone in bathing), she heard her father and mother talking in the sitting room. Father was adding up some accounts.

"The strawberries have done well," he was saying, "better than we expected. And the raspberries and blackberries are coming on. We can begin to buy a few of the things we need. Wasn't there a dress that you were going to have, dear, a silk dress? That was one thing that the strawberry money was for."

"I don't think I'll have that dress now," said Mother, in a voice which sounded a little queer.

"Why not?" asked Father quickly.

"I don't believe I really want it."

"Yes, she does," whispered Louise into her book. She knew that Mother wanted the dress dreadfully. She hadn't had any new clothes for a long time, and she wanted to go to the D. A. R. meetings in town, and visit Mrs. Sutherland, and make some calls.

"I'm sure you do want it," Father was saying.

"No, not now. There are so many other things," said Mother.

Louise knew that one of the "other things" was the Franklin stove that would make a bright fire for them to sit around, in cool autumn evenings. It was going to cost a great deal, but it would make them all happy when they had it. "Oh, dear!" said Louise to herself. She wanted Mother to have the blue silk dress that would go so well with her brown hair and pink cheeks.

"No, I don't think I'll have it, Gordon,"

said Mother. "Let's not talk about it any more."

"I don't know what I can say to change your mind," said Father, in a worried way. "I shan't let you give it up so easily. I shall keep at you every day."

"It won't be of any use," laughed Mother.

When Father had gone upstairs for something, Louise went into the sitting room. Mother was just lighting the lamp and the yellow light showed her face, calm and smiling, and not angry or sorrowful about the dress.

"I heard what you said, Mummy," said Little Girl in a low tone. "I think you should have the dress, because you need it and you want it."

"I don't mind," said Mother. "I'm happy enough as it is. Ssh—there comes Tall Father."

But a few days later something queer happened.

Louise was visiting Anna Fowler, and the two girls came into the house just as Anna's mother was looking in the sitting-room closet for her husband's rubber boots. It seemed that

Mr. Fowler had to mend a fence which ran through the marsh and the brook, and he needed the rubber boots to wear while he was working.

"I can't find them here," said Mrs. Fowler, who was busy baking pies, and did not like to leave them. "I believe they're up attic. Anna, won't you go up and see?"

"May I go along?" asked Louise.

"Why, surely," said Mrs. Fowler, going back to her pies.

So the girls climbed the stairs to the upper hall, and then climbed up another flight to the attic. At the ends were windows that did not light the corners nor the shadowy places behind boxes and barrels and old bedsteads. The rafters showed gloomy and dusty, and here and there a tiny crack between the shingles let in a thin ray of sunlight, which made a yellow line to the floor.

Anna found the boots standing near the stairs, but she lingered a little with Louise. "There's my doll's cradle," she said. "I had it when I was little. And there's the looking-glass I broke, throwing a ball. Mother's always going to buy a new glass, but she doesn't get around to it.'

Louise looked about at the jumble of things in the attic. She saw some lengths of stove-pipe lying in a dark nook. Then her eyes sharpened to the dusk, and she saw something else, which made her give a jump. It was a dark object—like a stove and yet not like a stove, for it was open in the front. "What's that, Anna?" asked Louise in a startled voice.

Anna answered, in a puzzled way, "Why, I don't know. It's some kind of an old stove, isn't it?"

"It's like a fireplace," said Louise, "only it's made of iron. Oh, I know, I know! It's a Franklin stove."

"A what?" asked Anna.

"A Franklin stove," said Louise, almost squealing in her excitement. "Whose is it, Anna?"

"Mother's, I suppose," said Anna. "What do you care about that rusty old thing?"

"I care a lot," cried Louise. She rushed downstairs ahead of Anna, forgetting to help her with the boots. "Oh, Mrs. Fowler," she said, bursting into the kitchen. "You know—that queer stove thing that you have in the attic——"

Mrs. Fowler was trimming the crust of a pie. "What thing?" she asked, looking perplexed.

Louise was dancing in her eagerness.

"Something like a stove, only it's open, and I think they call it a—a Franklin stove."

"Oh, yes," said Mrs. Fowler slowly. "I'd forgotten all about that." She was putting another crust into a pie tin.

"Do you want to keep it, Mrs. Fowler?" Louise could hardly get the words out. She felt shy and anxious.

"Why-y, I don't know as I do—or as I don't." Mrs. Fowler spoke carelessly, as if the stove were not of much importance. "I've never thought about it, I guess."

"Where did you get it?" asked Louise politely. Anna had come through the room with the boots, and was taking them out to her father, in the toolshed.

Mrs. Fowler poured some huckleberries into

her pie crust. "It was amongst the things Mr. Fowler's mother's folks brought out here from the East, years ago. I can't remember as it was ever used. It's been up attic ever since I had anything to do with the house. It's real old, I'm sure of that."

"Would—would you *sell* it?" asked Louise, catching her breath.

"Sell it!" Mrs. Fowler stood with a sugar scoop in her hand. "Who'd want the old thing? I'd have had it thrown away, long ago, except that it's so heavy to cart around."

"My mother wants one. She wants it *awfully*," panted Louise. She was so in hopes that Mrs. Fowler would let it go, if she did not care for it herself. It would be terrible if she wouldn't!

"Hm," said Mrs. Fowler, reaching for her flour sifter. "If anybody wants it, I'd like to see 'em have it, but I guess you're mistaken. I don't believe your mother wants anything like that."

"Oh, yes, she does; yes, she does!" cried Little Girl. "She told me so, a little while ago. I'm sure she'd love it."

"City folks are queer about old things,"
said Mrs. Fowler, as she cut out the top crust
for her pie. "You find out whether she really
wants it, though, and if she does, she can
have it—for nothing."

"Oh, no! I'm sure she'd want to pay you
for it, so you could get something you wanted.
That would be fair," said Louise earnestly.
She didn't want to take Mrs. Fowler's beautiful Franklin stove for nothing. She knew that
Anna's people had no more money than they
wanted, and she felt that they should have
some return even for the old stove in the
attic, that they didn't care about.

"Yes, that's fair," said Mrs. Fowler, smiling down at Louise in an odd way. "Well,
if she wants it, she can have it for five dollars,
but mind you, she's not to take it unless she
does want it."

"I know she does," said Louise, too much
pleased to say more. Anna came in just then,
with news of a baby calf in the barn and both
the girls rushed out to see it.

Louise could hardly wait till she got home,
but she didn't say anything to Mother about

the stove. She beckoned Father out into the woodshed, and told him all about it. "It's *just* what Mother wants," she explained excitedly. "She was afraid you'd feel sorry if you knew, and she was going to save all the money she could get, and buy one—so that we could have a fireplace in the sitting room, and all sit around it—Flora, and everybody."

"Hm," said Father, very much as Mrs. Fowler had done. "I didn't know anything about all that. And Mrs. Fowler will sell it?" he asked, after he had stood a while without saying anything.

"Yes, for five dollars. And can't you get it as a surprise for Mother? You may have all the money in my bank, to help, you know."

Father gave Little Girl a loving look.

"That's a fine idea," he said. "I'll tell you what—Mother's going to town to-morrow with Mrs. Rickman, and you and I'll go and look at this Franklin fireplace, and if it's all right, we'll buy it and bring it home, and set it up, and have a big surprise for Mother when she comes."

"Oh, oh, that would be too splendid for

anything," Louise burst out, jumping up and down.

"Can you keep from telling?" asked Father.

"Yes, honest, I can."

"All right. Not a word, Louella-Puella." Father was as pleased with their secret as a little boy.

They went back into the kitchen, where Mother was busy with some cooking, and Father gave Louella a knowing look, and Louella giggled and then straightened her face in a hurry.

"What are you two concocting?" asked Mother.

"Oh, we just have a little joke," answered Father, trying to seem indifferent.

The next afternoon, Mother went away in Mrs. Rickman's car, and Louise and Father were all agog over their plan for bringing home the iron fireplace. Father did not say anything about money, but Louise said to him before they got out Ann Eliza, "You said I might give some of my money for the Franklin stove, Poppy. You'll let me, won't you?"

"Yes, if you want to give it, Pet," said

Father. And very gravely he took a dollar and sixty-three cents from Louella—all the money in her bank.

"Some fathers wouldn't let their little girls give their money for a fireplace," said Louella; "but you will because you're so *understanding,* Poppy."

"Thank you, Little Girl," said Father. "I know just how you feel about it."

In a few minutes they were at Mrs. Fowler's house, and had climbed to the attic. Father pulled out his flash light and looked at the rusty and dusty old object under the rafters. "As sure as shooting, it's just what we want," he exclaimed. He and Mr. Fowler tugged and pulled, and brought the heavy thing down two flights of stairs, and somehow managed to get it into the car.

Father gave Mrs. Fowler five dollars. She laughed and said, "It seems foolish to take it, but Louise thought it wouldn't be 'fair' not to."

"She's exactly right," said Father, smiling happily. "What gives pleasure to us should give pleasure to you, too."

When they were out of sight of the house, Father waved his hat and shouted "Hooray," because he felt so delighted. And Louise shouted "Hooray," too, making a chorus for Father.

Father got Jerome Kingsley to help him get the fireplace into the house. It was a hard task, but after a while the Franklin stove was set up in the space between the door and the window, just where Mother would like to have it, and the stovepipe was in place.

"Why didn't we clean it before we brought it in?" asked Louise suddenly.

"I never thought of that!" said Father. He was wet with perspiration, and his face and hands were streaked with dust and soot. Louise ran to get papers and cloths and brushes and stove polish and brass polish. They worked "like tigers," as Father said, and in a little while the old fireplace looked as if it had never been out of Mr. Fowler's mother's parlor.

"Isn't it wonderful? Isn't it splendid?" Louise kept saying.

All this had taken a long time, and they were expecting Mother back at any minute. When Mrs. Rickman drove up, Father was hastily washing his hands in the kitchen, and Louise was hurrying to take the cloths and brushes and stove polish to the woodshed. The two plotters were in the sitting room when Mother came in through the front hall. Louise was jumping up and down with excitement, and Father was grinning and looking almost as shy and sheepish as a lad.

Mother had some parcels in her arms, and she was so busy with them and with kissing Louise that she walked right past the stove without seeing it. And then she turned around, and let all her parcels fall to the floor. "Why—why—what in the world?" was all she could say. "It's—it's a Franklin stove," she said at last, and her eyes were full of tears, and yet she was laughing, too. "Just what I wanted, more than anything else. Oh, Gordon, where did it come from? Is it ours—to keep?"

"Louise found it for you," said Father. He put his arm around Mother's waist, and they both stood and looked at the stove as if it were a beautiful painting or statue.

"Louise found it!" cried Mother in astonishment. "Where?"

"Just where it has been for years and years —in the Fowlers' attic," said Father.

And Louise told her mother, all in one breath, how she had seen the Franklin stove in the attic, and what she had said, and what Mrs. Fowler had said, and about the five dollars, and everything. "I wanted you to have it," she finished, "because you wanted one so much, and there isn't often anything that you just want awfully to have."

"She means, you don't often let anybody know what you want," added Father.

But Mother was kissing Louise, and saying, "You dear child."

"Now you can have the silk dress, after all," said Louise, who had just remembered.

"And that was why you wouldn't have it," said Father reproachfully. "Perhaps we could have arranged to have both."

"We can manage now," said Mother. "Thanks to our Little Girl."

"I didn't *do* anything, Mummy," said Louise. "I just *saw* the stove, and that was all there was to it."

"You're Mother's good girl," said Mother, and that was always the praise that made Louise the happiest.

Father had to burn a few papers and pieces of kindling in the fireplace, just to show how well it worked; but after supper a cool wind sprang up, and then the house was not too warm for a real fire on the hearth. It glowed yellow in the dusk of the unlighted room, and crackled and roared up the chimney. What a friendliness it gave to the sitting room! It threw a dancing light on the old painted clock, and the old china in the cupboard, and the chintz chair with the flowers and large-tailed birds on it, and on Mother with her arm around Louise and Father leaning over them. Flora came and lay down in front of the fire, and stretched out her dainty black-and-white paws—and then the picture was complete.

When she was undressing in her own pretty room a little later, Louise was thinking, "I've had a lot of things that I wanted, and Mother's had one thing that she wanted, and now I wish Father could have something that he wants.''

The days went faster than ever now, and the summer was getting shorter. The vegetables in the garden had grown large and vigorous, and they came to the table deliciously cooked by Mother's skillful hands. The sunflowers towered high above Louise's head, with their round yellow faces. The strawberries and currants and gooseberries had gone, and the blackberries and huckleberries had come, and the harvest apples were ripe.

It rained a good deal, and Louise and the other children played in the big barn or in the woodshed. Harry Fellows' mother and father were beginning to talk about going back to the city. Even school was not so far off that one need not think about it. One kept thinking, ''Only so many more weeks, and then school begins.''

One day Mother came in with the mail. She had been down to the store alone, and Father and Louise were in the woodshed, painting an old table that Father had bought at second-hand for a dollar. He was going to use it in his study, to keep his books and papers on, because they had a way of getting all over the couch and the floor.

Mother came running in through the living room and the kitchen. "Gordon, Gordon," she called, "here's a letter for you."

"I have had letters before, madam," called Father, but he knew this one was important. He wiped his hands on an oily rag, and went into the kitchen, Louise following. "Is it about the book?" he asked.

Mother nodded, handing him the envelope, which had the name of a New York publisher printed in the corner.

Father tore open the letter and read it through, with a queer look on his face.

"Oh!" said Mother, for she seemed to guess what the letter contained.

Then Father was smiling and dancing a jig. "Oh, ho! Oh, ho! Oh, ho!" he sang, jigging around and around. "What do you think? Oh, ho!"

"Is your book taken?" asked Mother, clasping her hands together, as she did when she was very much excited.

"Yes, it's taken, it's taken, oh, ho!" sang Father, whirling Mother and Louise around in his wild dance. "Aren't we a happy family now?" Mother hid her face on Father's shoulder. "Did you care so much, Honey?" he said.

"So much," answered Mother, "because you work so hard, Gordon, and you should have some reward."

"I'm having it now," laughed Father, and then he was sober again. "We don't know just how much this will mean—but it's a start, a fine start. Let us hope it will bring in bread and butter and sausages, at least."

"Now what will happen?" Louise had to ask, when she could get in a word. "Will they print all your typewriting into a book?"

"That's just what they'll do," said Father. He was reading the letter through again. "And every time anybody buys one of the books, I'll get a little money, and if a great many people buy a great many books, I'll get a great deal of money."

"Oh, I hope they'll buy millions," said Louise, picking up Flora and hugging her. Flora purred and rubbed her ears on Louise's chin.

"But there's more to it than that," said Mother. "It ought to be printed, because it's good, and you really had something to say."

"Well, I hope that's true," said Father. "And now, what can we do to celebrate?"

"Let's have a picnic," said Mother.

"And ice cream," said Little Girl.

"And a bonfire," said Father. "That's what they used to do in the old days to show how happy they were."

So Mother and Louise ran to pack a basket with good things, and Father ran to change his clothes and get out Ann Eliza, and in half an hour they were starting for a long ride around the lakes. They stopped at a stand near a big camping ground and bought ice cream packed in ice, and then they went on, to a quiet spot in the woods, on the shore of a clear lake which Louise had ridden through in the launch with the Fellows family. The

Martins were all by themselves, though they were not far from the road.

How they enjoyed the picnic, with Mother's nice sandwiches and salad and cake, and cold milk from the thermos bottle, and the pink-and-white ice cream!

"Nothing ever tastes so good indoors as it does at a picnic," sighed Mother.

"You don't get out enough," said Father. "I hope you will, after this."

"You know I *love* being at home," said Mother, patting Father's hand. "And not every one can be at home with a genius."

The most fun was the bonfire. They all carried armfuls of leaves and twigs and branches and pine cones, and piled them on a big flat rock at the edge of the lake. They worked until they had a huge pile, and more laid aside, to feed the fire when it should begin to fade.

Just as dusk was coming on, and the wind was getting cold, Father lighted his bonfire. "I'm going to have such a tall fire," said he, "that my publishers will see it, away off in New York, and they'll stick their heads out of the window and say, 'Well, Martin must be celebrating, out there in the Middle West. He thinks it's a big thing when we take his little book.' "

"It is a big thing, too," said Mother.

"And it's a big fire," said Little Girl.

The long, bright streamers of flame leaped up into the still evening air, and darted almost as high as the smaller trees. Sparks flew up and up, throwing their reflection upon the lake.

Louise and Father poked the fire with long sticks, and sent the flames and sparks still higher. When the ends of the sticks were burned to red coals, they whirled them round and round, making fiery wheels against the dark. When the fire died down, they built it up again, and it roared and leaped upon the solid rock, like some beautiful wild creature at play.

It seemed as if Father and Little Girl would never be tired of watching the flames, or of feeding them with twigs and branches. But after a while, Mother said, "It's getting late, children. We ought to be on our way."

Father looked at his watch. "You're right," he said. "Little Girl ought to be in bed this minute."

So they let the fire get lower and lower, and as its crackling stopped, they could hear the sounds of the woods—the chattering of raccoons, and the long, sad, quivering note of an owl. Across the lake came the sounds of singing and laughter, as a party of young people passed in a rowboat.

At last, Father carried some water in a pail and threw it on the red embers of the fire. They hissed and steamed and sank down into blackness. "Our celebration is over," said Father, "and thanking you one and all for your kind attention, we bid you good night."

They picked up all their belongings and got into the car. It was not easy following the wood road in the dark, but soon they were out on the main road, and Ann Eliza was carrying them home.

"We had a fine celebration about your book, didn't we?" said Louise happily and sleepily from the back seat, where she was cuddled against Mother's shoulder.

"We surely did, Pet," answered Father; but Louise was sound asleep.

Now the end of the summer was coming, and though Louise and Anna could still say, "No school to-morrow," there were not many days until school must begin again. They played in the barn and in the playhouse, and waded in the brook behind the foundry, and went in swimming down behind the store, and rode out in their fathers' cars, to make the most of every day as it came along. Mr. and Mrs. Fellows and Harry came to say good-by, because they were leaving for the city.

The last Saturday afternoon had come. Eddie and Anna and Bobby and Louise had romped all the afternoon in the barn and the orchard, and now they had wandered out beyond Father's land, to Mr. Calkins', where he had a little field of sweet corn and beets and carrots and cabbages. In the midst of the field, at the end of the corn rows and next to the cabbages, there was an old scarecrow, which had stood there all summer. Strangely enough, Mr. Scarecrow had not grown ragged in the storms and heat of summer, for his coat and hat were very good ones that had been put away for years in Mr. Calkins' attic—probably something that a minister had worn. The high hat and the long-tailed coat made the scarecrow look solemn and severe, as if he would like to tell the boys and girls to be good and work hard and study their lessons.

"Oo-oo, look at the scarecrow," cried Louise. It seemed as if he waved his arm, in its long sleeve, and beckoned them to come. "Let's play school," said Little Girl.

Laughing and shouting, they leaped over the low fence, and ran around the lonely, solemn scarecrow. "Let him be teacher," called Eddie, "and let the cabbages be the seats."

They all sat down on the big spreading cabbages, giggling and pushing, and acting like naughty children in school.

"Here are your books, boys and girls," said Eddie in a deep voice which was supposed to be the scarecrow's; and he tore off the outer leaves of a cabbage to give to the others for

"Let the scarecrow be teacher," called Eddie.

books, and kept one himself. "I want you to be able to read every word," he added.

Louise and Anna giggled some more—pretending to read their lessons out of the cabbage leaves, and Bobby, who had never been to school, looked puzzled, but cheerful. The scarecrow waved his sleeves and stood looking very stern, and the children "raised their hands" and snapped their fingers, and asked him foolish questions.

"Just think," said Anna, all at once, sitting back on her cabbage. "On Monday we really, truly go to school, and we're going to have a nice lady teacher, instead of a scarecrow."

"Why-y," said Louella-Puella, "I'd almost forgotten how it seems, but now I remember. *I like school.*"

"I do, too," said Anna soberly. "Vacation is nice, but school's just as nice, in another way."

"I'm glad we don't have to have a scarecrow for a teacher, or read out of cabbage leaves, and I know I'm going to love our school when it begins, day after to-morrow," said Little Girl.

CPSIA information can be obtained at www.ICGtesting.com
Printed in the USA
BVOW02s1925280715

410811BV00003B/76/P

9 781429 093651